Academic Freedom and Responsibility

Other titles recently published under the SRHE/Open University Press imprint:

Michael Allen: *The Goals of Universities*
William Birch: *The Challenge to Higher Education*
Heather Eggins: *Restructuring Higher Education*
Colin Evans: *Language People*
Gunnar Handal and Per Lauvas: *Promoting Reflective Teaching*
Vivien Hodgson *et al.*: *Beyond Distance Teaching, Towards Open Learning*
Peter Linklater: *Education and the World of Work*
Graeme Moodie: *Standards and Criteria in Higher Education*
John Pratt and Suzanne Silverman: *Responding to Constraint*
Marjorie E. Reeves: *The Crisis in Higher Education*
John T. E. Richardson *et al.*: *Student Learning*
Derek Robbins: *The Rise of Independent Study*
Gordon Taylor *et al.*: *Literacy by Degrees*
Alan Woodley *et al.*: *Choosing to Learn*

Academic Freedom and Responsibility

edited by

Malcolm Tight

The Society for Research into Higher Education
Open University Press

Published by SRHE and
Open University Press
Open University Educational Enterprises Limited
12 Cofferidge Close
Stony Stratford
Milton Keynes MK11 1BY

and
242 Cherry Street
Philadelphia, PA 19106, USA

First published 1988

British Library Cataloguing in Publication Data

Academic freedom and responsibility.
   1. United States. Higher education.
   Academic freedom
   I. Tight, Malcolm
   378′.121

   ISBN 0-335-09531-3

Library of Congress Cataloging-in-Publication Data

Academic freedom/edited by Malcolm Tight.
      p.   cm.
   Bibliography: p.
   Includes index.
   ISBN 0-335-09531-3
   1. Academic freedom – Congresses.   2. Education, Higher –
Congresses.   I. Tight, Malcolm.
LC72.A43   1988
378′.121 – dc19   88-18759 CIP

Typeset by Rowland Phototypesetting Ltd,
Bury St Edmunds, Suffolk
Printed in Great Britain by St Edmundsbury Press Ltd,
Bury St Edmunds, Suffolk

to b, f, h and s

Contents

Authors

Dr Malcolm Tight is Director of the Unit for Research in Part-time Higher Education at Birkbeck College, University of London.

Dr Ronald Barnett is an Assistant Registrar at the Council for National Academic Awards.

Dr Sinclair Goodlad is in the Department of Humanities at Imperial College, University of London.

Mary Hawkesworth is an Associate Professor in the Department of Political Science, University of Louisville.

Professor Guy Neave is in the Department of International and Comparative Education at the Institute of Education, University of London.

Professor Anthony O'Hear is in the Undergraduate School of Interdisciplinary Human Studies at the University of Bradford.

Professor Bhikhu Parekh is in the Department of Politics at the University of Hull.

Dr Margherita Rendel is in the Department of Human Rights and Education at the Institute of Education, University of London.

Professor John Turner is in the Department of Genetics at the University of Leeds.

1

Editorial Introduction

Malcolm Tight

This book has been commissioned and produced in advance of the 1988 Annual Conference of the Society for Research into Higher Education (SRHE), which takes 'Academic Freedom' as its theme, to serve as an introduction and thought-provoker for participants. The book also aims to be of more general and lasting interest to all involved in higher education, both in this country and overseas. With this general aim in mind, all the references given in the individual chapters have been collected together so as to form a basic bibliography at the end of the book.

Academic freedom is more of an issue in higher education today than it has been at any time since the student disturbances of the 1960s. Even a cursory reading of either the specialist trade papers or the quality national press is sufficient to reveal numerous mentions of the concept. These occur in a wide variety of contexts. One of the most publicized recent examples has been the dispute at Ruskin College, Oxford, involving the tutor David Selbourne, who has claimed that student protests over his writing in *The Times* (then in dispute with the trade unions) infringed his academic freedom. But many other cases affecting individual academics, and academics in groups, in their relations with their employers, their clients and their funders, appear with great regularity.

Other contexts in which academic freedom has been discussed recently include:
- the issue of free speech on campus, examples of its alleged suppression or abuse, and the consequences of the measures included in the 1986 Education Act which attempted to safeguard it;
- the effects of cutbacks in state funding on the ability of scientists to pursue research, the perceived injustices of assessments of research strengths and weaknesses, and the interference of funding bodies in the conduct of the research they commission or support;
- the impact of voluntary or compulsory redundancy measures, and the increasing prevalence of short-term contracts, on the ability of academics to continue their work.

Academic freedom also appears from time to time in the overseas news pages.

We read, for example, of the stultifying consequences of the central direction and control of academic life in Czechoslovakia; of the pressures placed on academics who express views contrary to those of the government in Singapore; and of the controversies surrounding the participation of delegates from South Africa in international conferences. And, most recently of all (at least at the time of writing – March 1988), there has been extensive reporting and analysis of the possible impacts of the current Education Reform Bill on higher education. There can be no doubt, therefore, that this volume is timely, although some may argue that it is a little too late.

The strategy which was taken in putting it together was to approach a limited number of practising academics who were known to have something interesting to say on the subject. The papers in this book should be seen as individual examinations of particular aspects of academic freedom. They are not position statements: plenty of those, issued by the various organizations involved in higher education, are already available.

Of course, in a volume of this size it has not been possible to cover specifically every aspect of the field. There might well have been, for example, separate chapters dealing with the perspectives of industry, science, the arts, research, students, the law, the public (polytechnics and colleges) sector, developing countries, etc. No apologies are made for these apparent omissions. All of the main themes are discussed in one or more of the main chapters included, and usually from a number of different angles. Taken as a whole, the book provides a useful complementary analysis of the subject as it affects western developed countries.

No dominant or common view of academic freedom emerges from the different chapters. Given the nature of academics and academic life – an area of endeavour which does not rate agreement very highly – this should not be at all surprising, even though the condition of academic freedom is central to that life.

In the chapter which follows this introduction, Anthony O'Hear expounds what might be termed a 'traditional' view of academic freedom. Quoting Newman and Leavis with approval, he argues for the restriction of academic freedom to universities; universities in this view being a particular type of institution, excluding many which operate under that title at the present time as well as the whole of the public sector. Within such universities, individuals meet, engage in 'useless' (i.e. not directly applicable) conversations and attempt to relate their academic specialisms to culture as a whole. O'Hear stresses the importance of the freedom to teach and to study, the role of the humanities and the need for scholarship to be conducted within a collegial environment. He argues that the maintenance of academic freedom implies a need for the long-term support of a certain number of qualified academics within autonomous institutions.

The next chapter offers a rather different view, set in an American context. Mary Hawkesworth begins by noting that threats to academic freedom come from within as well as without academe, and she illustrates this by giving examples of the continuing sexual harassment to be found in universities and colleges in the United States. There is, however, considerable resistance within these institutions to the development and implementation of policies designed to curb or remove sexual harassment, on the grounds that such policies themselves restrict the freedom of academics to express their opinions and pursue the truth. Hawkesworth argues that this stance rests largely on a belief in objective truth and the neutrality of knowledge, a belief which she extensively criticizes. Instead, she suggests an alternative conception of knowledge, one which regards cognition as a human practice and sees truth as subjective, mediated and contextual. Seen in this light, sexual harassment policies may themselves contribute to learning and understanding, challenging academics to evaluate their practices and their disciplines.

Guy Neave expands the scope of the discussion still further, providing a review of the changing interpretations of academic autonomy in western European countries. He starts by comparing two opposed medieval views of academic freedom, that of Bologna emphasizing the freedoms of students and that of Paris the freedoms of their teachers, and goes on to examine four alternative models of autonomy – the Kantian, in which state interference is permitted only in certain subjects; the Humboldtian, in which the state assumes a largely facilitating role; the Napoleonic, in which the great majority of decisions are made by the state; and the British, in which property-owning corporations of scholars are supported by the state but left to their own devices. Neave then considers the changes that have impacted on these models in recent years, first in the 1960s, when a greater degree of autonomy was granted to universities in many European countries, and latterly in the 1980s, when the state and its agencies have come to assert a more dominant role, making autonomy conditional on satisfactory performance. From the British point of view, the most revealing comparison is the extreme rapidity with which the move to conditional autonomy has been achieved in this country.

Sinclair Goodlad's approach to the topic is more internal and pragmatic. He focuses on the practice of higher education in the area of education for the professions, looking at teaching and learning methods, the curriculum and other aspects of the student learning experience. He emphasizes the underlying moral values upon which any interpretation of academic freedom is constructed, and suggests a framework in which theory and practice are balanced against the varying needs of individual and society. Using this framework, Goodlad goes on to identify four heresies which effect the prescription of curricula – determinism, academicism, utilitarianism and mechanism – and to advocate alternative practices, including reflection and consultation, problem-based work and engagement–reflection modes of study.

Bhikhu Parekh's concern is with the arguments that have raged in recent years concerning the perceived need for the universities to ensure freedom of speech on campus. The considerable publicity which has been given to politicians who have been invited to address campus societies, but have then been prevented from speaking by groups of students and others opposed to their views, has been reflected in a fierce debate between the advocates of 'no platform' and 'open door' policies. Parekh critically dissects these two positions, arguing that an open door policy is not sound because it conflates acceptance of *academic* discourse with the tolerance of any kind of discourse. He sees the 'no platform' policy, which would deny a hearing to those deemed to hold unacceptable or provocative views, as rather ineffective in that it ignores the wider realities beyond the campus while providing the conditions for the creation of martyrs within it. Parekh concludes that universities should open their doors to those willing and able to participate in academic life, with all that implies, but deny their platforms to those with other aims.

Margherita Rendel's chapter addresses the relationship between academic freedom and human rights in general, indicating the extent to which international accords provide a workable framework for governing the interchange between academics, their institutions and society. Interestingly, this analysis suggests that many of the freedoms claimed by academics may, at least to some extent, be applicable to other professional groups, and perhaps to the general population as well. Rendel argues that academic freedom is necessary for teachers and researchers if they are to be enabled to confer on society the benefits which stem from their work. She goes on to identify and discuss major recent ideological and financial attacks on academic freedom in the United States and the United Kingdom, stressing the cases of Marxism and Women's Studies, and notes the effects of these attacks in terms of self-censorship and other trends.

Ronald Barnett takes a very different view, stressing the manifold linkages which bind higher education within its host society and concluding that the notion of academic freedom, if this is taken to imply some separation of academics from society at large, is manifestly nonsense. He argues that academics have themselves acquiesced in binding their work into an ever closer relationship with society, seeking the benefits which came from additional resourcing and the expansion of the higher education system in the 1960s and early 1970s, and are thus in a poor position to complain now simply because of the current cutbacks in funding. He suggests that since academics tend to place most emphasis on their discipline or department, rather than their institution, and most students appear to have adopted a very instrumental view of the purpose of their studies, institutional autonomy may be a rather more pressing problem than individual academic freedom.

John Turner focuses on the recent debates surrounding the Education Reform Bill. He argues that neither the fuss generated over freedom of speech nor the antics of vice-chancellors are central to the notion of academic freedom, which remains a simple condition of work, designed to enable academics to pursue their investigations and make their criticisms without suffering adverse consequences in their employment. Though Turner concentrates on the threats to academic freedom stemming from the actions of the present government – through the abolition of tenure, the introduction of new funding arrangements and the taking of powers of direct intervention in institutional affairs – he also recognizes that many other bodies threaten academic freedom. He suggests that though academic freedom may not be cheap it is cheap at the price and its maintenance is essential if creative solutions are to be found to the many pressing problems facing society.

Finally, in the last chapter of the book I make an attempt to draw together the various insights provided by the other contributors, adding to them from the available literature on the subject, and to redefine the range of questions which have been posed. Ten basic questions are identified:

1 What are the values which underlie academic freedom?
2 What is academic freedom for?
3 Who gets academic freedom?
4 What is the position of students?
5 What is the relationship between academic freedom and institutional autonomy?
6 What is the relationship between academic freedom and general human rights?
7 What is the relationship between academic freedom and tenure?
8 What are the implications of all this for academic structures and practices?
9 What responsibilities does academic freedom confer?
10 What is academic freedom?

For some answers to these and other questions, please read on.

2

Academic Freedom and the University

Anthony O'Hear

Academic freedom, if it is to be distinguished at all from freedom of speech, cannot be discussed outside the context of the university, for it is a value which pertains directly to the university. At the same time, in considering the meaning of academic freedom we shall be led to draw a number of conclusions about the nature of the university as a special type of institution, with special duties and values.

Freedom of speech

There is a conception of academic freedom which hardly distinguishes it from freedom of speech. In this view, academic freedom amounts to no more than a right supposedly given to *academics* to say and teach what they believe to be true. Freedom of speech is, of course, a vital freedom which is denied to academics and others in many parts of the world, but there is nothing specifically academic about it. The right to say and teach what you believe is presumably something that friends of the open society would regard as being owed to journalists, lawyers, politicians, parents and, indeed, to people generally. It is not something which is at stake only or even primarily in academic life, although it is nevertheless peculiarly shocking when academics attempt to curtail freedom of speech – a point to which we shall return.

The dissociation of academic freedom and academic tenure that is readily insisted on by politicians, university administrators and newspaper leader writers comes largely from a conflation of freedom of speech and academic freedom. In this view, not paying or continuing to employ a tenured academic would not be interfering with academic freedom, if the sacking were not for directly ideological reasons. After all, it would be said, sacking a few people from a university does not interfere with the freedom of the rest to say and teach what they believe. Nor, indeed, does it interfere with the freedom of expression of those sacked. No one at the University of Surrey is going to be beaten up for holding a philosophy seminar, even if they are no longer paid for it.

Although lack of tenure can interfere in subtle (and not so subtle) ways with an academic's freedom to teach and research as he sees fit, there is a clear distinction to be drawn between freedom of speech and academic freedom, along the following lines. Freedom of speech is the right someone has within certain limits not to be interfered with in his or her expression of thought. In other words, freedom of speech is basically a freedom *from*, in the freedom-from/freedom-to distinction. Academic freedom, on the other hand, looks much more like a freedom *to*, which we can see if we consider the case of an academic ordered by his institution to work in the administration or the car parks all day long. Most people would think of this as a denial of academic freedom – the freedom *to* teach and research as the academic sees fit. This freedom-to clearly requires much more from the academic's employing institution than just the lack of interference implied by freedom of speech. It implies at least a long-term commitment on the part of the institution concerned to provide conditions in which the academic can teach and study.

Academic freedom and research

There is another view of academic freedom which, though open to criticism, does relate it to security of academic employment rather more than the freedom of speech notion. On this view, academic freedom is regarded as a means to a worthwhile end, not as either a necessary or a sufficient means, but as a means nonetheless. The end would be variously described as the making of important discoveries, doing of creative work and the like. The idea is that academic life and academic freedom should exist so that the boundaries of knowledge and experience can be pushed back in some way. Undeniably this is one aspect of academic life, though hardly its whole aim.

Part of the difficulty here comes from the vagueness in talk of important discoveries and creative work. To take two examples of research recently undertaken in a university: is finding out something about domestic lighting practices in Britain or about the school meals service of Inner London important? – Important in some ways, no doubt, but *academically* important? And would research of this sort justify giving the academics concerned *academic* freedom and the security of tenure associated with it rather than, say, short-term contracts for the duration of the research and commensurate with its potential and success? Further, as many people have pointed out, very little artistically creative work goes on in universities, and even in the sciences the returns in terms of what scientists regard as crucial theoretical discoveries seem miniscule for all the work and resources that go into universities. Newman was both correct and prescient when he pointed out in the Preface to *The Idea of a University* (Newman 1852) that there are 'other institutions far more suited to act as instruments of . . . extending the boundaries of our knowledge than a university.' He was correct because, as we shall see, a university has a crucial role to play in the life of a society which does not involve extending the boundaries of knowledge. He was prescient because taking that to be the central purpose of a university is one of the main reasons for our current distorted view of the university, and the resulting bias in the assessment of institutions in terms of their research 'productivity'; something which distorts the true aim of the university itself, and of research too in many cases.

A university dean once told me that he valued academic tenure even if its only benefit was that it allowed just one out of three hundred academics to produce something really important. In addition to the implied contempt for the efforts of the other two hundred and ninety-nine and the problems involved in knowing whether it was someone's tenure that was crucial to his producing his important discovery, one could surely propose more cost-effective ways of running scientific and other types of research if that is one's aim. One could (as Newman suggests) set up high-powered research institutes or academies whose sole aim was research. What is wrong with the dean's view is that it is based on a very narrow view of a university, which fails completely to take into account the cultural and educative role of the university, and hence to see that academic freedom, and even tenure, might be an important aspect of university life and university education, apart from the way in which academic freedom might or might not benefit research results.

University education

There is a vital educational and cultural task which universities, and only universities, are especially suited to undertake. This task will need for its successful execution a specifically academic freedom, meaning by that something which is more than freedom of speech, and something which is not aimed simply at providing an environment for successful research work or justified in terms of research results.

The educational and cultural task which I have in mind for the universities is, in the words of F. R. Leavis:

> to explore the means of bringing the various essential kinds of specialist knowledge and training into effective relation with informed general intelligence, humane culture, social conscience and political will. Here in this work we have the function that is pre-eminently the university's; if the work is not done there it will not be done anywhere.
>
> (Leavis 1979, p. 24)

Part of the point of doing this will be the educational one of bringing aspiring specialists into such an effective relation, of putting them in a position to see what the relationships might be between their specialism and informed general intelligence, humane culture, social conscience and political will.

Leavis is, of course, expounding the vision of the university which Newman adumbrated in his Dublin discourses on university education delivered in 1852. Newman sees the rationale for grouping students and teachers from diverse disciplines together in one institution as being the production in individuals of that 'true enlargement of mind which is the power of viewing many things at once as one whole, of referring them severally to their true place in the universal system, of understanding their respective values, and determining their mutual dependence' (*Discourse V*). A liberally educated man – the ideal product of the university – will possess knowledge 'not only of things, but of their mutual and true relations': he will see the particular discipline in which he specializes in terms of its place in the whole of knowledge, and in the way in which it contributes to and is suffused by that whole.

Newman is very far from opposing a deep knowledge of one particular discipline. Indeed, he believes firmly that 'a smattering in a dozen branches of study' is shallowness, a dissipation of mind rather than progress or true education. A rigorous immersion in one particular branch of study is a real education of the mind, but what is wanted over and above that – which may remain at the level of mere learning, useful to others maybe, but not to its possessor – is the wisdom that comes from the possession of a connected view and grasp of things. Newman distinguishes this cast of mind from what he calls 'viewiness', that tendency to the instant production of an opinion on any subject whatever, which is the province of journalism and the mass media and which journalism and the mass media foster. The critical methods of university disciplines ought to enable one to resist temptations to this sort of viewiness, while it is Newman's hope that contact with teachers of one's own discipline who have sympathy and communion with scholars from other disciplines, together with contact with students from other disciplines, will help to produce in the minds of those studying in universities 'the calm, clear and accurate vision and comprehension of all things, as far as the finite mind can embrace them, each in its place, and with its own characteristics upon it.'

It is no doubt unfashionable to see the aim of any sort of education as the cultivation in the minds of the uninitiated of a sort of wisdom, as opposed to skills, techniques, information or money-earning capacities. But Newman is unashamedly platonic about education, seeing its end in the improvement of individual minds. He would entirely have accepted the point of Socrates's warning in the *Phaedrus* (274C–275B) about the invention of writing on the grounds that the written word can be anti-educational. Writing will lead men to rely on external marks rather than on knowledge they have properly assimilated and taken into their hearts. Such men, the precursors of today's information technologists, will know nothing themselves and have the conceit of wisdom, rather than wisdom itself. According to Socrates these conceited empty-heads will be a burden to their fellows; certainly they will have repudiated any sense of the true point or worth of knowledge, as contributing to one's wholeness and sensitivity as a human being. And Newman's vision of the university is that it should be an institution fostering the development of individuals of a certain type. This, to repeat, is the rationale for having different disciplines and scholars, teachers and students all grouped together under one roof.

According to Newman, the way a university might help to produce the philosophic cast of mind he seeks will be largely through the tradition and atmosphere of a place in which the cultivation of the intellect is valued for its own sake. In such a place, there will be teachers versed in the various disciplines who are at the same time in some sort of collaborative contact with those in other disciplines, and pupils or students from different places and backgrounds. Such an institution will define its own interrelationships, establish its own rules, and gain its own tone and character:

> It will give birth to a living teaching, which in the course of time will take the shape of a self-perpetuating tradition, or a *genius loci*, as it is sometimes called; which haunts the home where it has been born, and which imbues and forms, more or less, and one by one, every individual who is successively brought under its shadow.
>
> (Newman, *Discourse V*)

It is true that Newman does not say enough about just which disciplines will be represented in his university. In the ninth *Discourse*, rather in the spirit of Kant, he speaks of God, Nature and Man being the three great subjects of human reason, though he then goes on to exclude revealed theology from the scope of his discussion, which he restricts to the physical and social worlds as revealed through science and literature respectively. But, rather surprisingly, he says nothing there about either history or philosophy as separate disciplines, although in his Preface to the *Discourse* he had spoken of grammar, mathematics, history, chronology, geography, poetry and philosophy as being important stages in any intellectual training. However, more important than the details of Newman's own curriculum is the spirit in which studies will be conducted in his university. There will no doubt be literary, historical, scientific, philosophical, psychological and sociological studies undertaken, but they will not be under- taken in a narrow way. What is required is not that every academic and every specialist should regard the explorations between his specialism and the rest of culture as his or her *primary* task, but rather that they should recognize the importance of that task and be ready to conceive their specialism ultimately in terms of its bearing on culture as a whole. The ideal is high and difficult, no doubt, but aiming at it is not only the main reason for grouping separate subjects under one roof, it is also the only way in which teaching and research can steer a humane path between the Scylla of dried-up pedantry on the one hand and the Charybdis of technological manipulation on the other.

If universities are to be centres for the cultural task being suggested here, academic freedom, which I will now define as the freedom of qualified academics to teach and research in a secure environment, is highly desirable, if not practically indispensable. This is because the task is one that requires both mature and disinterested reflection and some commitment to the ethos of the university as a focus of collaborative endeavour and teaching. It is not a task that can properly be undertaken by people under pressure to publish, to 'attract' students, to be relevant to the 'needs' of industry, to come up with quick research results, etc. The deleterious effects of such pressures on academic work have often been noted and I will say no more about this here. But insofar as the task I am envisaging as the *raison d'être* for the university as a special type of institution is one which is in itself different in kind from, if not actually critical of, the evaluation of everything in terms of production and consumption, people whose teaching is supposed to be aimed at producing another type of wisdom in their students are hardly likely to convince them of its importance if in their own work they are themselves obviously motivated by the values of educational consumerism – quantities of publications, ability to 'attract' students, to get outside money, and the rest. All of these considerations would be quite in order if the university were a market-orientated institution, but to see it as such is to miss its actual *raison d'être*, and will lead to the destruction of such universities as actually exist.

'Actually existing universities'

The university envisaged by Newman is an institution in which conversations of a certain sort – about truth, beauty and goodness – will not simply be *possible*. Such conversations are always possible, even, one is almost tempted to say, in present-day universities. In Newman's university, though, conditions will be such as to *foster* such conversations, and the conversations will be between those disciplined and expert in the various central fields of human knowledge, and between people aiming to become so disciplined and expert. Academic freedom, envisaged as the freedom to teach and research, is crucial to those teaching in such an institution because they will otherwise be subject to pressures which will take them away from their central task, particularly the pressures to specialize narrowly and to serve various short-term ends, economic and political.

Newman's ideal university is very much a Socratic one. We have, though, to recognize that Socrates was never employed by the city of Athens. If our cities see virtue in having institutions devoted to a Socratic type of conversation and education, we may justifiably claim to have advanced beyond Athens in at least one respect. But the city will have to pay the cost, and resist the temptation to interfere. Athens put Socrates to death; our problem is whether we can resist suppressing the university ideal. Looking at 'actually existing' universities in this country, one wonders whether the city is any longer capable of the self-denying ordinance necessary to support a true university. The city is generous enough with its money, but it cannot bring itself to let the money just go to those whose vocation it is to run the university. And even worse, academics, whose vocation it is to foster the life of the university, and whose security of tenure is predicated on the basis of that vocation, continually show themselves ignorant of its meaning.

Specialization

Reading Newman, one gets the impression that the whole whose parts are the various specializations is easy to construct, or, rather, with Newman, that the whole is already divinely ordained. For Newman's vision of the unity of knowledge was sustained and informed by his Catholicism. Lacking divine guarantees of the ultimate coherence of our world and our culture, the task of relating the different parts of what we know to each other and to the rest of our lives is at once more difficult and more urgent. Specialization is the way many choose to avoid the task altogether.

Leavis, indeed, writing in 1943 saw specialization as a problem not merely for the university:

> But the academic world is part of the contemporary world, and the university itself has been disabled for the task by the process which makes the task so urgent: the idea of liberal culture has been defeated and dissipated by advancing specialization; and the production of specialists . . . tends to be regarded as the supreme end of the university, its *raison d'être*.
>
> (Leavis 1979, p. 25)

If the idea of liberal culture has been so completely defeated, though, then we can stop pretending to have universities. The so-called binary divide in higher education is wiped out at a stroke, and we can settle down to what many see as the really important task of discovering the most cost-effective ways of running scientific research on the one hand and higher education in specialist skills on the other, without being shackled by the belief that there is some virtue in having a lot of different subjects grouped together in the same institution.

Science and humane culture

In considering university education, it is crucial to distinguish between the nature of the study of the physical world, on the one hand, and that of the human world, on the other, and to see that the methods of the one cannot be assimilated to the methods of the other. In scientific study, what we are concerned with are the natural essences of things, meaning by that their underlying structure and potential for causal relationships. The success of a scientific theory depends entirely on its ability to predict and explain the behaviour of natural phenomena. In so doing, it will pay no attention to the way things affect us or to the meanings they might have for us, and may actually show us that the way things appear to us distorts their true nature. All questions of human meaning and value are or should be excluded from the theories of science, precisely because they attempt to explain and describe a world we envisage as having an existence and nature independent of human activity. For this reason, we cannot *within* science treat the meaning or significance for us of scientific knowledge. This question is one which belongs to the human world, and one for which scientific study on its own does not prepare us.

The human world, by contrast to the physical world, is one which is constituted by the ways things affect us as human beings, and the ways our responses and lives have been historically structured. While all this is in some fundamental sense constrained by our biology, the surface structures and forms of our lives are historically conditioned. Questions of meaning and value are of the essence here, and it is in the historical, literary and philosophical disciplines that they are most directly treated, in explaining the roots of our values and institutions, in describing their felt significance for human subjects and in considering their validity. Social science and science generally may well give us data we will have to take into account in considering the human world, but they will not themselves provide us with the means of reconstructing how things might actually feel to human agents or of actually evaluating meanings and interpretations that agents place on their activity. The sciences, including the social sciences so far as they are actually scientific, necessarily prescind from judging questions of value and significance. I cannot go into any more detail on this point here (although I do in my book, *The Element of Fire* (O'Hear 1988)). But it should be clear enough that the Leavisite task of bringing specialist knowledge and training into effective relation with general intelligence, humane culture, social conscience and political will is one that requires active liaison between specialist disciplines in various fields, and the humane centre of the university constituted by its humanities departments. For this reason, a university without the disciplines of history, literature and philosophy cannot be a university, however prestigious an institution it may be. It is only through those disciplines that the human significance of the various specialisms and of our lives and institutions can be properly explored, although it is also unfortunately true that the work of teaching these disciplines is all too often conducted without any regard for human significance.

Science and freedom of speech

Despite all the current commotion about saving British science, if I were a scientist I might fear for my job but I would not be seriously perturbed about the future of science. For one thing, the very notion of 'British' science is a curious one, at least for those who have grasped the point made in the previous section about the a-human and a-cultural perspective of science. While one might intelligibly fight to save British music or British literature, I am not clear what, beyond jobs, one is fighting for in attempting to save British science. Apart from this all governments all over the world now accept that science provides the goods people want, so that they will be extremely loathe to curtail its progress in their country. In addition, rulers are by now all so thoroughly intimidated by the stories of Hitler failing to get the bomb because of his repudiation of 'Jewish' science, and of the disastrous economic effects of Lysenkoism in the USSR, that they are not seriously going to interfere on political grounds with freedom of scientific thought within their jurisdiction (only left wing councils in this country can afford that sort of luxury, and then only at the elementary school level). Because of their prestige and wealth-creating potential, scientific research and training hardly need charters guaranteeing their freedom. What those concerned with academic freedom in the university should worry about, though, is the way the ethos of a university can be distorted when the values and monetary claims of scientific specialisms and research projects come to dominate its deliberations and plans, and when the quest for profitable research results, proper to an institute of technology, comes to seem the aim of the university itself.

Business studies and the needs of the economy

The distortion brought about in a university by the influence of scientific specialisms is due to the fact that these specialisms are often materially useful. They can issue in profitable technologies, which provide a cogent and tangible reason for government and industry to give financial support to their projects and researches. Problems for universities arise when such wealth-creating activity is seen as the be-all and end-all of a scientific department, and its proper place within the whole corpus of knowledge forgotten. But science at least has a genuine contribution to make to the corpus of knowledge, even if its centrality to the economic development of a country means that scientific study and research can normally get along very well without having to appeal to any notion of academic freedom or the values that academic freedom is designed to foster.

On the other hand, it could hardly be said that management and business studies perform any vital contribution to what we know about man and his place in nature. This point is amusingly if unintentionally brought home by the way in which Sir Peter Swinnerton-Dyer, the Chairman of the University Grants Committee (UGC), proclaims that university departments of Business and Management require a 'critical mass' of 40 academics because of the numbers of disciplines involved in such studies. Such departments are in fact simply training schools for management, and live off fruits from other trees of knowledge. While there can be no objection to such schools in their proper place, it is quite unclear why they should exist in universities, or why people working in them should enjoy the specific academic freedom which involves their having tenure. Those who live by the market should, if the occasion arises, be allowed to die by the market. Instead, all too often their very existence in a university means that, in unholy alliance with technology departments, they contrive to produce a market ethos in an institution which should by its nature be resistant to such an ethos.

Political activism and the university

Academic freedom is necessary to protect the university ethos of civilized and humane conversation, by which the various kinds of specialist knowledge and training can be brought into effective relation with general intelligence and humane culture. Particularly in an atmosphere in which our knowledge of the world, the soul and God is not underwritten by a strong religious faith, the characteristic modality of the conversation will be the 'It is so, isn't it?' of the literary critic, where one expects in reply the 'Yes, but' of finer distinction and discrimination.

It is nothing short of scandalous that the present Government has had to legislate in order to try to preserve free speech in our universities, but hardly surprising given that some university departments are full of political activists, who have no commitment to the value of free speech, let alone to the ethos of the liberal university, represented by full academic freedom. Just as much as the incursion of market values in the university, the tentative, questioning, conversational, critical-collaborative spirit of the university is subverted by curricula which presuppose the correctness of a particular political point of view, and by academics who use the cloak of academic freedom to mask the true nature of their distinctly illiberal activities. These activities can be all the more harmful in the context of a university in that the politicized academic often indulges in a type of posturing and attitudinizing found fascinating and seductive by the young. One is reminded by such academics of Heidegger's Rectoral Address of 1933, in which the youth of Germany is told to commit itself to a mass movement which holds the future in its hands. 'The time for decision is past', Heidegger said, 'the decision has already been made by the youngest part of the German nation.' The fact that a real thinker could say such a thing in such a context (Bloom 1987) serves only to show how vulnerable the university is to *trahisons des clercs*, when academics bring their political convictions, which they have every right to express outside the university, into their teaching. The life of the mind is necessarily individual and necessarily – for the time at least – disengaged from causes; part of the true function of the university is to make its pupils – for a time at least – stand back from causes, and – for a time at least – engage in thought rather than in action.

Useless conversations

It is precisely because universities are useless institutions that they need academic freedom. To the extent that they are useless economically and politically, university teachers may make a justifiable claim on the security of tenure implied by academic freedom. To the extent that they see their role in terms of economic or political usefulness, there seems no reason for them to be granted more than the freedom of speech that members of other trades and professions can rightly claim. Useless universities need academic freedom as part of their ethos precisely to make possible the sort of useless conversations and education that too much looking over one's shoulder at economic or political circumstances will make impossible. But these useless conversations are actually the most important of all, for it is only in such conversations that one comes to realize what it is to be a human being and that one comes fully to be a human being, sharing in the sacred rage and at times even the shame which Alcibiades experienced in listening to Socrates. I say this because what the university should be about above all is understanding man and his place in nature: from the point of view of the university the real point of the various specialisms is the contribution they can make to the self-understanding of each one of us.

I do not know what hope there is for the university as Newman envisaged it. I am pretty sure that the only hope for an institution devoted to the life of the mind is that it should be self-regulating and allowed to develop organically, at at least one remove from extraneous pressures. Extraneous pressures are certainly being brought to bear on universities at the moment, pressures to conform to the market and to judge university activities by market criteria, and these pressures are corrupting both of the spirit of the university and of academic freedom. But equally corrupting to the spirit of the university was the expansion forced politically on universities in the 1960s, where a different type of relevance was sought and numbers of ill-judged decisions were once again made on grounds that were academically quite spurious. The rot really set in in the wake of Robbins, for it was borne in on universities then as never previously that they were to be perpetual suppliants at the hands of governments. Whether the government is prodigal or penny-pinching is hardly the point once genuine university autonomy is undermined. One must not forget that the rhetoric of universities serving the needs of the economy was one firmly established in the Robbins report, and universities happily went along with it then. To that extent we are even now still reaping the harvest sown by Robbins.

But, it will be said, we in universities must surely bow to economic reality. Surely universities must be relevant in some sense to the world in which they exist, and which supports them? But here we have to insist once again that universities can really serve the society that supports them only by resisting 'economic reality' and – through their commitment to a genuine notion of academic freedom – by standing for a different view of the relationship between economics and society. To quote Leavis again:

> A university of its very nature, if it is one at all, asserts a contrary view of cultural tradition to the Marxian: a view of cultural tradition as represent-ing the active function of human intelligence, choice and will; that is, as a spiritual force that can direct and determine.

(Leavis 1979)

In this society, few of us are Marxists and yet, in a sense, we all are, in our reduction of everything to the economic. Universities should represent a countervailing force in the present climate. They should stand for the Idea of the University and for the academic freedom which that entails. If they so do they will be worthy of public support and of the freedom they claim for themselves. If they do not, they need to bring forward a view of what the university is which is at least as cogent as that propounded by Newman.

3

The Politics of Knowledge: Sexual Harassment and Academic Freedom Reconsidered

Mary Hawkesworth

Both the moral and intellectual integrity of Western universities are under fire, from within and from without, by those who would politicize, moralize, or deform an institution whose primary allegiance is to cognitive rationality, to disciplined search for truths.

(Chapman 1983, p. 1)

Whether the intellectual heritage of the concept is traced to Socrates' maieutic art, to the norms of the twelfth century *universitates* in Bologna and Paris, to the nineteenth century German conceptions of *Lehrfreiheit* and *Lernfreiheit* or to the ideals of twentieth century academics struggling to achieve professional autonomy, discussions of academic freedom typically invoke the notion of a quest for truth (Hofstadter and Metzger 1955). The multiple dimensions of academic freedom – the freedom to teach, research and publish without interference, the right to exercise civil and political liberties without endangering academic status, and the demand for academic control over the content of the curriculum and the conditions of employment (especially in terms of hiring, tenure and promotion) – acquire their legitimacy in the context of the exigencies of the search for truth.[1] The difficult and time-consuming process of generating and validating knowledge claims affords a justification for the insulation of scholars from untoward pressures both in the process of discovery and in the dissemination of ideas. Because the truth may be unpopular, challenging received views in multiple and systematic ways, those who bear its message must be protected from political and economic reprisals. Because universities are committed to the advance of knowledge and because assessment of knowledge claims requires expertise, decisions concerning what will be taught and by whom must be left to the competent judgement of faculty in determinate disciplines.

If the dimensions of academic freedom derive from the demands of the pursuit of truth, so too threats to academic freedom can be understood as derailments of that quest. In contemporary society, the dangers which imperil universities lie within as well as without academia: in the use of power – political, economic or ecclesiastical – to truncate inquiry, to suppress unorthodox views, to prescribe a curriculum or to dismiss dissenting faculty; in the imposition of management techniques and norms of productivity foreign to the academic enterprise; in the deployment of standards incompatible with scholarly excellence in the evaluation of faculty performance; in the ascendancy of the instrumental conception of education which renders academia subservient to the short-term interests of the public and private sectors; and in the reign of the research contract which threatens to erode academic objectivity and disciplinary integrity (Carnegie Foundation Report, 1982; Chapman, 1983; Kaplan and Schrecker, 1983; Pincoffs, 1975).

   The purpose of this paper is not to investigate all potential threats to academic freedom, but rather to remove one particular kind of academic self-regulation from the category of the threatening. My particular concern is to refute claims that the development and implementation of sexual harassment policies constitute a violation of academic freedom. Toward that end the paper will take the following form. The first section will consider the problem of sexual harassment within the university and the means by which remedies to that problem generate claims concerning infringements of academic freedom. The second section will examine certain assumptions concerning truth, objectivity and power which sustain the charge that sexual harassment policies curtail academic freedom. Drawing upon recent work in epistemology and the philosophy of science, the third section of the paper will suggest that the epistemological assumptions which inform traditional defences of academic freedom are fundamentally flawed. A review of the character of these defects will suggest that the pervasive acceptance of these assumptions impairs rather than advances the quest for truth by truncating inquiry, removing important questions from the sphere of legitimate investigation and masking the politics of knowledge. The paper will conclude with a discussion of an alternative conception of knowledge, a conception which suggests that policies which heighten sensitivity to issues like sexual harassment facilitate critical inquiry and hence foster rather than infringe academic freedom. Due to the limitations of space, I shall concentrate on the issue of sexual harassment in the context of American higher education. I believe, however, that these arguments have implications beyond the borders of the United States and that they are pertinent to the development of policies prohibiting racial and ethnic harassment as well as sexual harassment within the university community.

Sexual harassment

Although the practices associated with sexual harassment have a long history, they have been acknowledged as a form of unethical conduct and as a manifestation of illegal sex discrimination only in the past ten years.[2] Within the university, unwelcome sexual advances, requests for sexual favours and other verbal or physical conduct of a sexual nature constitute sexual harassment when: (1) submission to such conduct is made either explicitly or implicitly a term or condition of an individual's employment or academic achievement; or (2) submission to or rejection of such conduct by an individual is used as the basis for employment decisions or academic decisions affecting such individuals; or (3) such conduct has the purpose or effect of unreasonably interfering with an individual's work or academic performance or creating an intimidating, hostile or offensive working or academic environment.

In contrast to the stereotype which conflates sexual harassment with overt sexual propositions as a condition for employment or successful completion of a course, sexual harassment includes a range of verbal as well as physical behaviours. Physical harassment may range from leering, fondling and pinching to rape. Verbal harassment occurs in the form of persistent derogatory comments pertaining to a person's sex. For example 'I didn't expect you to follow what I said. It's well known that women are incapable of higher reasoning.'; or 'You really ought to switch your field of study to literature. A woman trying to master mathematics might as well try to grow a beard.'; or 'You'll have to face the facts – there's no room for women in the world of engineering. The demands for strength, rigour and precision are simply more than any woman can muster.' Verbal harassment may also take the form of sexist remarks which draw attention to a person's body, clothing or sexuality. For example 'With a body like that, you don't need to study.'; or 'Although it's obvious from your disposition that it must be that time of the month, could you trouble yourself to answer this question?'; or 'Your presence in this classroom is unnecessary. Nature has ordained that women's fundamental role is that of reproducer of the species; any other undertaking is purely superfluous.' Utterances of this sort constitute sexual harassment precisely because they create a hostile and intimidating environment which impairs women's academic performance.

A number of studies have documented that verbal sexual harassment, whether in the form of graphic commentaries on the victim's body, degrading descriptions of the victim's sex or overt sexual propositions, adversely affects the victim's mental and physical health and undermines the victim's self-esteem (Dziech and Weiner 1984; Farley 1980; MacKinnon 1979).[3] The consequences of sexual harassment upon an individual's academic aspirations and educational achievements are just beginning to be investigated (Hall and Sandler 1982, 1984, 1986). One study at the University of Illinois indicated that 18.7% of the students who had experienced sexual harassment on campus suffered a marked deterioration in academic performance; 23.4% altered their course selections in order to avoid the harasser; and 13.9% of the victims changed their major area of study and their career plans in order to escape further harassment. A similar study at Harvard University revealed that 12% of the undergraduate students and 15% of the graduate students who experienced sexual harassment altered their academic objectives as a result of the harassment (Dziech 1987). A ten-year study of 80 high school valedictorians (i.e., those who graduate first in their class) also indicated that universities afford a far less hospitable environment to women students than to men and that this difference has palpable effects on women's career choices. Although female valedictorians typically outperformed their male counterparts academically throughout their college years, as early as the second year of university; 'two-thirds of the women began reporting lower levels of intellectual self-esteem and less ambitious career aspirations than they did when they graduated from high school' (Denny and Arnold 1987).

As a form of sex discrimination, sexual harassment ensures that women do not experience educational opportunities on the same terms as men. They confront obstacles, exploitation and insult solely because of their sex. The perniciousness of sexual harassment is matched by its pervasiveness. The study at Harvard University indicated that 32% of the tenured women faculty, 49% of the untenured women faculty, 41% of the female graduate students and 39% of the female undergraduates had experienced sexual harassment at Harvard. In the United States, it is estimated that 20–30% of women students are subjected to sexual harassment during their university studies (Epstein 1981; Hall and Sandler 1986, p. 10).

In response to the problem of sexual harassment (and in response to court cases which have held universities liable for sexual harassment)[4], a number of universities have developed sexual harassment policies which condemn sexual harassment as unethical and unprofessional conduct, prohibit its practice and establish procedures for investigation of complaints and punishment of harassers.[5] Among the prohibitions included in such policies is a proscription from the classroom of all derogatory comments pertaining to a student's sex.

It is this provision which provokes the charge that sexual harassment policies violate academic freedom. Taking the freedom to teach to imply an absolute right to say anything in the classroom, some faculty have argued that the prohibition of sexist insults constitutes an unacceptable abridgement of academic freedom; others have suggested that acceptance of censorship in this domain would open the door for the imposition of restrictions upon political speech, ideological views or unorthodox scientific claims; others have warned that allowing courts or government administrators to dictate acceptable norms for classroom material threatens the very notion of academic autonomy.[6] Thus the critics suggest that however well-intentioned sexual harassment policies might be, they cannot be tolerated for they subject scholars to unwarranted social pressures; they introduce standards for judging academic performance that are unrelated to intellectual excellence; they threaten economic reprisals against those who articulate an unpopular 'truth'; and they jeopardize the autonomy of the profession.

Are these charges valid? Are they defensive reactions of harassers seeking to shield their behaviour from scrutiny? Are they expressions of legitimate concern by scholars seeking to protect the classroom from politicization? Rather than psychologizing these allegations and imputing motives to those who advance them, I would suggest that it is possible to gain a fuller comprehension of their merits if they are understood as predictable manifestations of prevailing epistemological assumptions. The conceptions of truth, knowledge, and rational inquiry which pervade American higher education sustain the critique of sexual harassment policies as violations of academic freedom. To assess the validity of these charges, then, it is important to consider the nature and the adequacy of these epistemological assumptions.

Objective truth and neutral knowledge

The belief that the tools of rational inquiry are neutral, that the principles of logic, the strategies of rational analysis and the methods of scientific investigation are value-free, is widely accepted in the American academic community. Reflecting the legacy of the Scottish Enlightenment, American pragmatism and positivism, these beliefs support a strain of empiricism which has influenced norms of competence, criteria of expertise and standards for appropriate interaction between faculty and students in the classroom. Indeed, it has been suggested that these beliefs have played a central role in shaping the American conception of academic freedom itself (Hofstadter and Metzger 1955, pp. 400–406; Chapman 1983, pp. 5–7).

Whether incorporated in logical positivism, logical empiricism, analytic philosophy, critical rationalism or materialism, mutually reinforcing empiricist assumptions provide a formula for the preservation of the objectivity of scholarly investigations and for the insulation of research from the taint of bias.[7] That formula requires the dichotomous division of the world into the realm of the 'empirical' and the realm of the 'non-empirical'. Structured in accordance with the belief that knowledge is dependent upon the evidence of the senses, the empirical realm comprises all that is amenable to corroboration by the senses; as a residual category, the non-empirical comprises everything else. On this view, as long as scholarly investigations operate within the realm of the empirical, eschewing speculative and valuative discourse, objectivity lies within reach. The division of the world into separate spheres and the restriction of valid cognitive inquiry to the sphere of 'facts' provides a means for the maintenance of objectivity and the attainment of truth.

Reliance upon a public methodology lies at the heart of this conception of intellectual objectivity. Through adherence to neutral analytic or scientific methods, the subjectivity of the scholar can be controlled. Moreover, claims of truth resulting from the use of public methodologies can be subjected to verification through intersubjective replication. Thus the inquiries of an individual researcher can be distilled to the operation of pure reason through a process of hypothesis formulation, deduction of empirical consequences, testing predictions against empirical events and intersubjective corroboration or falsification of results. Those claims which withstand repeated intersubjective tests can be tentatively accepted as true.

On this view, intellectual objectivity is understood in terms of intersubjective testability or intersubjective corroboration. Yet to avoid the conflation of objectivity with consensual or conventional justification, this strain of empiricism relies upon the correspondence theory of truth. The correspondence theory of truth holds that a statement (proposition, idea, thought, belief, opinion) is true if that to which it refers (corresponds) exists; thus the truth lies in correspondence with facts. A neutral, public methodology is crucial then, not only because it allows intersubjective corroboration of truth claims, but also because it enables diverse inquirers to grasp things as they are, to experience facts in their immediacy.

Once the validity of truth claims has been established, they can be included in the ever-increasing category of the known. The accumulation of such claims constitutes the existing body of knowledge within determinate disciplines. Demonstrated mastery of such objective knowledge affords the criterion for genuine expertise within a scholarly field. Dissemination of such knowledge becomes the responsibility of the scholar within the classroom. On this view, education consists neither in indoctrination nor in the inculcation of values, but rather in the exposition of objective knowledge, certified as true by a consensus of competent experts within the discipline.[8]

Assumptions concerning the neutrality of scholarly inquiry provide a justification for particular research methodologies, a practical mechanism for the determination of truth, a criterion for legitimate academic authority and a standard for appropriate faculty behaviour in the classroom. They also afford an immunity against claims concerning the problem of sexual harassment. On this view, faculty acting in accordance with the principle of neutrality neither indulge nor tolerate value-laden judgements concerning sexuality in the classroom, hence sexual harassment policies are unnecessary. In disciplines which require classroom discussion of sex, gender or sexuality, faculty operate in conformity with the norms of objective inquiry and advance claims on the basis of their expertise and in light of existing knowledge. In these cases, prohibitions concerning sexual harassment are dangerous, for they threaten to curb the exposition of objective knowledge. Moreover, sexual harassment policies, whether promoted by university administrators or by faculty from other disciplines, interfere with established procedures for validating truth claims and, as such, jeopardize disciplinary autonomy in specific instances and undermine the principle of academic autonomy more generally.

From the perspective of those imbued with an understanding of the neutrality of the scholarly endeavour, sexual harassment policies stand as a formidable menace. The scope of the menace is directly related to unquestioned assumptions about the reasonableness, feasibility and authority of a particular conception of knowledge. If the neutrality of the academic, the objectivity of knowledge claims and the related rejection of prohibitions against verbal sexual harassment are inextricably linked to the validity of this conception of objective knowledge, then an examination of the adequacy of these epistemological presuppositions is essential for an adjudication of the charges against sexual harassment policies.

Cognition as a human practice

Recent work in epistemology and the philosophy of science has challenged the notion that a neutral scientific or philosophical method can render subjectivity nugatory in the process of investigation. Critics have suggested that the notion of a value-free methodology affording an objective grasp of reality depends upon conceptions of perception, experience, knowledge and the self which are problematic. Critiques of foundationalism[9] have emphasized that the belief that there is a permanent, ahistorical, Archimedean point which can provide a certain ground for knowledge claims is incompatible with an understanding of cognition as a human practice (Albert 1985; Bernstein 1983; Cavell 1979; Rorty 1979). They have suggested that the belief that particular techniques of rational analysis can escape finitude and fallibility and grasp the totality of being misconstrues both the nature of subjective intellection and the nature of the objective world. Attacks on foundationalism therefore raise questions concerning specific forms of knowing, particular conceptions of subjectivity and various theories of the external world. Insights drawn from these works can illuminate inadequacies in the epistemological assumptions which inform the academic critique of sexual harassment policies.

Standard critiques of foundationalism question the adequacy of both deductive and inductive logic as the ground of objective knowledge. To challenge rationalists' confidence in the power of logical deduction as a method for securing the truth about the empirical world, critics typically point out that the truth of syllogistic reasoning is altogether dependent upon the established truth of the syllogism's major and minor premises. Yet when one moves from relations of ideas governed by logical necessity to a world of contingency, the 'established truth' of major and minor premises is precisely what is at issue. Thus rather than provide an impeccable foundation for truth claims, deduction confronts the intractable problems of infinite regress, the vicious circle or the arbitrary suspension of the principle of sufficient reason through appeals to intuition or self-evidence (Hume, 1748; Albert, 1985).

Attacks on empiricist exuberance have been equally shattering. It has been repeatedly pointed out that inductive generalizations, however scrupulous and systematic, founder on a host of problems. Observation generates correlations which cannot in themselves prove causation. Conclusions derived from incomplete evidence sustain probability claims not incontestable truth (Albert 1985; Popper 1962). Moreover, where rationalism tends to overestimate the power of theoretical speculation, empiricism errs in the opposite extreme by underestimating the role of theory in shaping perception and structuring comprehension. Thus, the objectivity of the empiricist project turns upon the deployment of an untenable dichotomy between facts and values, a dichotomy which misconstrues the nature of perception, fails to comprehend the theoretical constitution of facticity and uncritically disseminates the 'myth of the given' (Sellars 1963; Winter 1966; Bernstein 1976; Gunnell 1986).

As an alternative to a conception of knowledge which is dependent upon the existence of an unmediated reality that can be grasped directly by observation or intellection, anti-foundationalists suggest a conception of cognition as a human practice (MacIntyre 1981). On this view, knowing presupposes involvement in a social process replete with rules of compliance, norms of assessment and standards of excellence which are humanly created. Although humans aspire to knowledge of the world in itself, the nature of perception precludes such direct access. The only access available is through theory-laden conventions which organize and structure observation by according meanings to observed events, bestowing relevance and significance upon phenomena, indicating strategies for problem-solving and identifying methods by which to test the validity of proposed solutions. Knowledge, then, is a convention rooted in the practical judgements of a community of fallible inquirers who struggle to resolve theory-dependent problems under specific historical conditions.

Acquisition of knowledge occurs in the context of socialization and enculturation to determinate traditions which provide the conceptual frameworks through which the world is viewed. As sedimentations of conventional attempts to comprehend the world correctly, cognitive practices afford the individual not only a set of accredited techniques for grasping the truth of existence, but also a 'natural attitude', an attitude of suspended doubt with respect to a wide range of issues based upon the conviction that one understands how the world works. In establishing what will be taken as normal, natural, real, reasonable, expected and sane, theoretical presuppositions camouflage themselves, blurring their contributions to cognition, masking their operation upon the understanding. Because the theoretical presuppositions which structure cognition operate at the tacit level, it is difficult to isolate and illuminate the full range of presuppositions informing cognitive practices. Moreover, any attempt to elucidate presuppositions must operate within a hermeneutic circle. Any attempt to examine or to challenge certain assumptions or expectations must occur within the frame of reference established by mutually reinforcing presuppositions. That certain presuppositions must remain fixed if others are to be subjected to systematic critique does not imply that individuals are prisoners trapped within the cognitive framework acquired in socialization.[10] Critical reflection upon and abandonment of certain theoretical presuppositions is possible within the hermeneutic circle; but the goal of transparency, of the unmediated grasp of things as they are, is not. For no investigation, no matter how critical, can escape the fundamental conditions of human cognition.

The conception of cognition as a human practice thus challenges the possibility of an unmediated knowledge of the world, as well as notions such as 'brute facts', the 'immediately given', 'theory-free research', 'neutral observation language', and 'self-evident truths', which suggest that possibility. Because cognition is always theoretically mediated, the world captured in human knowledge and designated 'empirical' is itself theoretically constituted. Divergent cognitive practices rooted in conventions such as common sense, religion, science, philosophy and the arts construe the empirical realm differently, identifying and emphasizing various dimensions, accrediting different forms of evidence, different criteria of meaning, different standards of explanation, different tokens of truthfulness. Such an understanding of the theoretical constitution of the empirical realm in the context of specific cognitive practices requires a reformulation of the notion of 'facts'. A 'fact' is a theoretically constituted proposition, supported by theoretically mediated evidence and put forward as part of a theoretical formulation of reality. A 'fact' is a contestable component of a theoretically constituted order of things (Foucault 1973).

The recognition that all cognition is theory-laden has also generated a critique of traditional assumptions concerning the subject/self which undergird rationalist, empiricist and materialist conceptions of knowing. Conceptions of the 'innocent eye', of the 'passive observer', and of the mind as a *tabula rasa* have been severely challenged (Popper 1962; Brown 1977; Stockman 1983). The notion of transparency, the belief that the individual knower can identify all his/her prejudices and purge them in order to greet an unobstructed reality, has been rendered suspect. Conceptions of the atomistic self which experiences the world independent of all social influences, of the unalienated self which exists as potentiality awaiting expression and of a unified self which can grasp the totality of being have been contested (Benhabib 1986; Taylor 1984; Connolly 1985). The idea of the 'subject' has been castigated for incorporating assumptions of the 'logic of identity' which posits knowers as undifferentiated, anonymous and general, possessing a vision independent of all identifiable perspectives (Megill 1985; Young 1986). Indeed, the very conception of the knowing 'subject' has been faulted for failure to grasp that rather than being the source of truth, the subject is the product of particular regimes of truth (Foucault 1977, 1980). In post-modernist discourses, the notion of a sovereign subject which possesses unparalleled powers of clairvoyance which afford direct apprehension of internal and external reality has been supplanted by a conception of the self as an unstable constellation which is produced by the complex interaction of a multiplicity of unconscious desires, fears, phobias and conflicting linguistic, social and political factors (Moi 1985).

In addition to challenging notions of an unmediated reality and a transparent subject/self, the conception of cognition as a human practice also takes issue with dichotomous accounts of reason which privilege one particular mode of rationality above all others. Attempts to reduce the practice of knowing to monadic conceptions of reason fail to grasp the complexity of the interaction between traditional assumptions, social norms, theoretical conceptions, disciplinary strictures, linguistic possibilities, emotional dispositions and creative impositions in every act of cognition. Approaches to cognition as a human practice emphasize the expansiveness of rationality and the irreducible plurality of its manifestations within diverse traditions. Perception, intuition, conceptualization, inference, representation, reflection, imagination, remembrance, conjecture, rationalization, argumentation, justification, contemplation, ratiocination, speculation, meditation, validation, deliberation . . . even a partial listing of the many dimensions of knowing suggests that it is a grave error to attempt to reduce this multiplicity to a unitary model. The resources of intellection are more profitably considered in their complexity, for what is involved in knowing is heavily dependent upon what questions are asked, what kind of knowledge is sought and the context in which cognition is undertaken (Cavell 1979).

The conceptions of neutral knowledge and value-free methodology which pervade American higher education are markedly defective. They fail to recognize that perceptions are theoretically mediated, that facts are theoretically constituted and that methods of inquiry are permeated by value-laden assumptions concerning the objects of inquiry.[11] Recognition that value-laden theoretical presuppositions organize and structure research by according meaning to observed events, identifying relevant data and significant problems for investigation and indicating both strategies for problem-solving and methods by which to test the validity of proposed solutions requires the abandonment of the myths of neutral knowledge and of value-free inquiry. It does not require abandonment of conceptions of truth and objectivity. That there can be no appeal to neutral, theory-independent 'facts' does not imply that all theoretically mediated knowledge claims are equally valid. The conception of cognition as a human practice suggests that it is possible to make and warrant critical evaluative judgements concerning claims about the internal and external world. But it insists that all such judgements operate within the limits of fallible human cognition.

In the absence of claims of universal, ahistorical validity, rational judgements derive their justificatory force from their capacity to disclose and illuminate dimensions of physical and social experience, to demonstrate the deficiencies of alternative explanations of the same phenomena, to debunk opposing views. In the context of specific research questions, reflective judgements concerning truth depend upon rational argument, upon a systematic demonstration of the cogency and coherence of a particular argument, coupled with a detailed demonstration of the defects of contending interpretations.[12]

The politics of knowledge

The conception of cognition as a human practice has important implications for our understanding of education. To begin with, it suggests that education involves immersion in established traditions of cognition. In order to acquire knowledge students accept the authority of that tradition and the tutelage of its practitioners. The authority exercised by faculty in the classroom involves far more than the objective exposition of neutral ideas. In the process of teaching, academics shape students' understandings of social processes, interpersonal relationships and human possibility. Intentionally or not, faculty impart to students accredited modes of existence as well as sanctioned modes of thought.

Moreover, the conception of cognition as a human practice suggests that the canons of received truth incorporate theoretical presuppositions which are biased in unsuspected ways. Thus, even when consciously adhering to norms of neutrality and objectivity in the classroom, scholars will disseminate theory-laden and contentious views. For this reason, proponents of cognition as a human practice suggest that rather than assume that one methodology is sufficient to ensure the validity of knowledge claims, scholars must ask multiple questions concerning the level of analysis, the degree of abstraction, the type of explanation, the standards of evidence, the criteria of evaluation, the tropes of discourse and the strategies of argumentation deployed in investigations of concrete problems. Awareness of the structuring power of tacit theoretical presuppositions requires detailed investigation of the political implications of determinate modes of inquiry. Questions concerning the politics of knowledge form a legitimate area of inquiry, for the analytic techniques developed in particular cognitive traditions may have a determinate political cast.

Awareness of the human origin of cognitive conventions has important implications for university education in particular. On this view, faculty have a responsibility to teach students more than the official canon. They must cultivate in their students a capacity for critical reflection. Students must be taught to examine the processes by which knowledge has been constituted within determinate traditions and to explore the effects of significant omissions (such as the experiences of women and minorities) upon those traditions. Students must be taught to investigate the adequacy of the standards of evidence, criteria of relevance, modes of analysis and strategies of argumentation privileged by the dominant traditions. Recognition of the theoretical constitution of the empirical realm requires an expansion of the research agenda: scholars and students must examine the presuppositions which circumscribe what is believed to exist and identify the mechanisms by which facticity is accredited and rendered unproblematic.

In raising critical questions, challenging received views, refocusing research agendas and searching for methods of investigation adequate to the problems of humanly constituted truth claims, the conception of cognition as a human practice offers strategies of inquiry designed to illuminate tacit bias in the established disciplinary canons. In so doing, it illuminates several problems rendered invisible by the fundamental commitments of the empiricist tradition. For those committed to the notions of value-free knowledge and neutral methods of inquiry simply cannot explain the persistence of sexist bias in the traditional doctrines of humanities, social science and natural science disciplines (Harding 1986). Nor can they explain how 'neutral knowledge' disseminated in a value-free fashion can have a differential impact on male and female students. They can shed no light on the gradual erosion of self-esteem among women students who maintain excellent academic records.

When considered in the context of cognition as a human practice, arguments supporting sexual harassment policies acquire a new force. A recurrent theme among proponents of sexual harassment policies is that faculty need not consciously intend to demean and insult women students, to curb their career objectives or to circumscribe their life prospects. On the contrary, by tacitly incorporating the norms of sexist society in their jokes, asides, examples and authoritative assertions about their subject matter, faculty may *unwittingly* curtail the aspirations of their students. Sexist values may be so deeply entrenched in the received and accredited views of the world, that the nature of the insult contained in a 'good-natured joke' may be altogether invisible to the joker. Similarly, the derogatory character of references to women in literary, philosophical and scientific discourses may be imperceptible to faculty convinced of the neutrality of their scholarly researches. Behaviour informed by sexist assumptions may produce *unintentional* discrimination. Different modes of interacting with women students, different standards of assessment applied to women's academic performance, different levels of attentiveness to the questions and comments of women students, different expectations and reinforcements for women's achievements, and different degrees of supportiveness for women's endeavours may be an unconscious characteristic of faculty activity. Sexual harassment policies are important, then, not only because they protect the educational opportunities of women students, but also because they sensitize faculty to the possibility of tacit bias, they heighten awareness of the complexity of truth claims and they stimulate on-going critical reflection. Seen in this light, sexual harassment policies may spur faculty to consider the political dimension of allegedly neutral academic discourses. By serious and systematic reflection upon the manner in which seemingly innocent statements may create a hostile and intimidating academic environment for women, faculty may come to recognize and remove the pervasive distortions about women which permeate the dominant disciplines. Where the myth of a neutral method blinds faculty to the possibility of sexism, sexual harassment policies counsel continuing scrutiny of cognitive conventions. In this way, sexual harassment policies themselves contribute to the quest for truth.

If my thesis is correct, sexual harassment policies which press faculty to consider tacit bias within their disciplines simultaneously challenge deeply entrenched epistemological assumptions. It would not be surprising then that the development of such policies would meet with impassioned resistance. Yet, however intense this resistance may be, it should not be allowed to prevail. For those who would repudiate sexual harassment policies by appealing to principles of 'neutrality', 'objectivity' and 'cognitive rationality' are themselves establishing an unwarranted prohibition against rational inquiry. They are attempting to remove important issues concerning the politics of knowledge from the sphere of legitimate scholarly investigation. When one considers that the justification for this intellectual ban depends upon epistemological assumptions which have been severely challenged, if not altogether discredited, the legitimacy of this proscription is undermined.

Discussions of academic freedom typically focus on power as a constraint upon academics: political, ecclesiastical or administrative power used to constrict legitimate scholarly pursuits or to curb important academic prerogatives. It is far less common to hear discussions of the constitutive powers of academics within the classroom, discussions of teachers' power to produce disciplined subjects, that is, to produce students whose minds and bodies have been disciplined in order to mould their capacities, improve their performance, increase their utility and docility and thereby integrate them into the prevailing system of control (Foucault 1977, 1980). An additional benefit of sexual harassment policies is that they alert faculty to such power relations in the classroom. Sexual harassment policies ask teachers to consider the constitutive character of disciplinary socialization and to explore the political cast of diverse cognitive practices. They ask faculty to ponder their possible complicity in the dissemination of sexist bias, in the perpetuation of discrimination. Sexual harassment policies do not threaten academic freedom. Rather, they challenge academics to confront their power to produce a world in their own image and in so doing force academics to assume responsibility for the freedom they exercise in the university setting.

Notes

1 Ellen Schrecker has suggested that the first two dimensions of academic freedom, which she conceives in terms of rights of individual academics, are not necessarily compatible with the third, which she conceives as a collective right pertaining to the autonomy of the academic profession as a whole. Indeed, Schrecker argues that to ensure the protection of the third dimension, i.e., to free hiring, promotion and curricular decisions from outside interference:

> . . . the academic profession took upon itself the task of policing itself and making sure that none of its members would do anything to bring about such intervention . . . the academy has come to exclude from the realm of scholarship those individuals, activities and ideas it feels may endanger the profession's autonomy.

To support her case, Schrecker provides a detailed account of the firings of academics during the McCarthy era, not only for affiliations with the Communist party but merely for invoking the Fifth Amendment and refusing to testify about colleagues. (In Kaplan and Schrecker 1983, pp. 25–43).

2 Arguments that Title VII of the 1964 Civil Rights Act and Title IX of the 1972 Educational Amendments could provide the statutory basis for the prohibition of sexual harassment as an illegal form of sex discrimination were first aired in the late 1970s in the United States. In 1980, the Equal Employment Opportunity Commission issued guidelines (29 CFR Chapter XIV, § 1604.11 [a-f]) calling for the establishment of appropriate sanctions for sexual harassment.

3 The studies reviewed in these texts have documented that women exposed to sexual harassment suffer insomnia, head, neck and backaches, stomach ailments ranging from nausea to ulcers, decreased concentration, diminished ambition, depression, fear, anxiety and feelings of being trapped and defeated.

4 In 1977 in *Alexander* v. *Yale University*, a Connecticut court ruled that Title IX of the 1972 Educational Amendments requires that universities develop institutional procedures for responding to sexual harassment complaints.

5 In a study of 668 American universities conducted in 1983–4, Claire Robertson found that two-thirds had a written sexual harassment policy and that 46% had grievance procedures specifically designed for sexual harassment complaints. For full details of this study, see Robertson (1985).

6 Such claims were advanced by members of the faculty of the College of Arts and Sciences at the University of Louisville in the course of debating the propriety of amending the Code of Faculty Responsibilities to include a prohibition against sexual harassment. Similar arguments were raised by faculty at the University of Toronto and by faculty of Cornell University in response to draft sexual harassment policies in those institutions. Although I have not been able to locate any data indicating the frequency with which these claims are raised, Billie Dziech confirmed my suspicion that concerns about academic freedom surface regularly in response to proposed sexual harassment policies. As one of America's foremost experts on sexual harassment in educational institutions, Dr Dziech has spoken on the topic on college campuses across the United States. She reports that she regularly encounters

objections concerning abridgement of academic freedom from faculty. It should be noted, however, that the American Association of University Professors (AAUP), the official guardian of academic freedom in the United States, has condemned sexual harassment in the University community as 'deplorable and illegal'.

7 There are, of course, important differences among these diverse epistemological views which I do not mean to deny or underrate. For the purposes of this analysis, what I wish to emphasize is that these various epistemological positions share an excessively simple conception of knowledge, of the relation between the knower and known and of the mechanisms by which knowledge can be accredited. Thus, despite their differences, I believe these diverse positions are vulnerable to the criticisms detailed in this chapter.

8 Such a role for the educator might appear to suit the scientist far more satisfactorily than the philosopher. Yet this standard has been applied to faculty in all disciplines. Consider, for example, the policy statement of President Harper of the University of Chicago who stated categorically that: 'A professor is guilty of an abuse of his privilege who promulgates as truth ideas or opinions which have not been tested scientifically by his colleagues in the same department of research or investigation' (*President's Report* December 1900). Compare the arguments concerning the nature of education advanced by President Eliot of Harvard University: 'Philosophical subjects should never be taught with authority. They are not established sciences; they are full of disputed matters, open questions, and bottomless speculations. It is not the function of the teacher to settle philosophical or political controversies for the pupil, or even to recommend to him any one set of opinions as better than any other. Exposition, not imposition of opinions is the professor's part.' ('Inaugural Address,' *Educational Reform* (New York: 1898; pp. 7–81)). For a discussion of the pervasive acceptance of this conception of education within the American academic community, see Hofstadter and Metzger (1955) pp. 320–412.

9 As an epistemological strategy, foundationalism attempts to identify an infallible 'ground' for human knowledge, a permanent, ahistorical ground which can validate human knowledge claims.

10 In *Beyond Objectivism and Relativism*, Bernstein characterizes this erroneous conclusion as the 'myth of the framework.' p. 84.

11 In contrast to empiricism's benign description of its methods in terms of value-neutrality, Wolin (1981) has argued that empiricist methodology is more accurately understood as 'mind engaged in the legitimation of its own political activity.'

12 It is impossible to provide a full defence of the coherence theory of truth which underlies this position within the confines of this paper. For discussion of the coherence theory of truth, see Bernstein (1983); Cavell (1979); Connolly (1981); Gunnell (1986); and Herzog (1985).

4

On Being Economical with University Autonomy: Being an Account of the Retrospective Joys of a Written Constitution

Guy Neave

Introduction

'Autonomy', said the Minister for Research and Higher Education 'does not mean total liberty, for indeed there are as many forms of autonomy as there are facets in the life of the university.' (*Council of Europe Newsletter* 1986).

With hindsight, it was a daring and unhappy statement. And true though it might be, the infelicitous phrase did not prevent M. Devacquet's sudden departure to the roar of an amazing number of French students and to the undoubted relief of his ministerial colleagues. It was yet another example of Kipling's Law of Political Behaviour – losing your head while all around you keep theirs!

Now the point of this vignette is not to illustrate the fickleness of cabinet solidarity nor the ingratitude of students. The point is , rather, to suggest that it is not only in the United Kingdom that accepted notions of 'university autonomy' are under siege. The difference between Britain and France resides in the fact that the defence of the established order was conducted rather more vigorously in the latter than in the former country. And, no less significant, that defence was conducted by the student estate on the streets rather than by heads of establishments rolling in the corridors of power. *Avec les résultats que l'on sait* . . .

Yet the fact that both the British and French governments are bent on revising certain aspects of university life which the university world, whether staff or students, holds to be central to the notion of 'autonomy' cannot escape the equally evident fact that what is understood by 'university autonomy' is very different in France and Britain. And, just as their concept differs from ours, so we are apt to interpret theirs in the light of our own norms. In short, autonomy is contextually and politically defined. A key element in both instances is the role of the state – or, if I were to take a French view on the British situation up to recent times, its absence. From the standpoint of much of the Anglo-American literature dealing with higher education in western Europe, academic autonomy there is set around with top-heavy, bureaucratic control exercised by central administration. Or, to paraphrase Burton Clark, control and co-ordination are vested in the upper layers of the system in the Ministry of Education or, in the case of France, the Ministry of Higher Education and Research (Clark 1984). The shared assumption which runs across the Anglo-American interpretation of academic autonomy *à l'Europénne* is that central control over student numbers, conditions of access and entry, staff appointments and a high degree of budgetary dependence on state finances (98.4% of the total income of West German universities in 1983 came from state sources, 90% of French universities' income in 1982 and 92% for Swedish universities in 1984–5 (Neave 1987a)) are both dysfunctional and pose severe limitations upon what would otherwise be a broader concept of autonomy.

They are dysfunctional because they prevent individual institutions from taking a more adventurous and flexible response to what are deemed society's changing needs. They prevent individual initiatives. In short, academic autonomy is held in thrall to a massive and insensitive technocracy whose sole loyalty is to the legal circular, the Ministerial decree and the maintenance of system uniformity by formal means. In essence, the Anglo-American view of autonomy Continental style can be summed up as 'the more extensive the laws, the less academic autonomy.' Nor, truth to tell, is this view exclusively Anglo-Saxon. A recent study, designed to *measure* the degree of autonomy in certain western European systems of higher education, reached the conclusion: 'In a given country, the weaker academic autonomy the more it is mentioned in legislative texts.' (Jadot 1984, p. 284) But does this mean that autonomy is at its greatest when unspecified or when subject merely to various forms of unspoken conventions between the powerful and the consenting, often alluded to as 'gentlemen's agreements'? This, as recent British experience and the wit of George Bernard Shaw, ought to remind us, is risky. 'The English gentleman always plays fair. Until he loses. And then he changes the rules of the game.' And this, the less charitable might say, is precisely what, over the past few years, he has been busily doing in the name of the national interest!

It is clear that, over the past six years or so, the issue of academic autonomy has come to the forefront of the battle between higher education and government. Not all countries are engaged in so stark a revision as one sees in the United Kingdom. Nor, necessarily, is the dialogue of discourse couched in so abrupt a manner. Presentations may differ. In France, change in this area is put forward as part of a wider drive to decentralize the country's administrative institutions. A similar theme emerges in the Netherlands, though one can also detect overtones not very dissimilar to those found in the United Kingdom. *Autonomy and Quality* and *Higher Education and Research Planning* are the titles of discussion documents put out by the Netherlands Ministry of Education and Science in 1984 and 1987 (von Vught 1987). In Spain, the Law on University Reform, passed in 1983, brought about considerable revision in the relationship between central government and universities. In addition, it created a new administrative layer at the regional level, thereby increasing the power of regional interests to be represented in academia in the shape of the Social Council installed in each university (Carreras, 1987, p. 77).

Placed against this background, the spate of reports and recommendations which have issued forth from Jarratt, Croham and the recent Education Act appear as a specifically British response to what is, in essence, a major European phenomenon. However, it is not my intention to diminish the significance of the British experience by putting it in one corner of a broader canvas. There *are* aspects of current reforms in the United Kingdom which depart radically from what appears to be the general thrust of reform in Europe. Broadly speaking, the official justification for change in the three countries just mentioned is to move away from close oversight of central administration and give some latitude to individual establishments to develop their own initiatives. It remains to be seen how successful the Spanish reform will turn out to be, though there, too, as in France, student resistance has been evident. Nevertheless, in the case of both France and Spain the intent of government is to move away from the Napoleonic model of the university. In Britain, the trend appears to lie in the opposite direction. By this, I do not mean the rise of central direction by circular or Ministerial decree, but the creation of a number of reserve powers that may be exercised by the Secretary of State. Essentially, this involves the state setting down the outer limits within which university autonomy may be exercised and, as such, may – at least from a comparative perspective – be interpreted as taking Britain along the road towards a concept of autonomy more in keeping with a model found in western Europe than, for instance, the type of relationship predominant in the United States. If this is so, then the changes through which the United Kingdom is passing are revolutionary for two reasons: first, because they stand to alter the fundamental theory on which university–government relationships have been based; second, because for the first time they afford an explicit and legitimate role to the State. From a European standpoint, the latter could be regarded as bringing Britain into line with practices long established on the mainland. Be this as it may, the time is ripe to take a closer look at the various forms of autonomy that exist – and have existed – in western Europe, and to examine their justification.

Models of autonomy

It is, of course, an historical cliché to say that the origins of university autonomy go back to the foundation of that institution in the twelfth and thirteenth centuries. There were, however, two major models: that of Bologna and that of Paris. Each represented a very different type of autonomy which related to different constituencies. In the Bologna model, the notion of autonomy applied to the student constituency. It consisted in the freedom of the individual to learn. The Paris model, by contrast, viewed autonomy as the freedom to teach and applied primarily to academe, of which students were a subset, rather than academe as the employees of students. The medieval concept of autonomy was part of a rather broader underpinning of contemporary social organization, grouped around guilds or corporations, each of which enjoyed various privileges or exemptions in the practice of their activities. They owned property and, like other guilds, exercised control over those admitted after due apprenticeship to their ranks, as well as a high degree of self-government. Their independence and, eventually, their right to interpret scripture, relied considerably on the protection of the local ruler. In other words, university autonomy owed much to the conflict between princes and prelates or, in certain instances, like the municipal University of Amsterdam, to the determination of the city fathers to demonstrate *their* independence from the Prince by founding their own establishment.

By the mid-eighteenth century, this pattern of organization, inward-looking and in a phase of high decadence, had become marginal to the activities of scholarship and devoted largely to the perpetuation of established orthodoxies. The impulse for reform did not, however, come from within the university so much as from despots of varying degrees of enlightenment, anxious to modernize the apparatus of the state by creating an administration based on formal competence and formal qualification. Nowadays, we tend still to identify the rise of the modern university with the work and thought of Wilhelm von Humboldt on the one hand and, for those specializing in the countries of a Roman tradition, of the Emperor Napoleon on the other (Neave and Rhoades 1987, p. 257).

In fact, the process of incorporating the university to the service of the State was well under way elsewhere – in Sweden between 1720 and 1772 (Svensson 1982) and in Austria under Maria Theresa and Josef II (Gruber 1982). Neither in Austria nor in Sweden was the process of linking the mission of the university to the state accompanied by any major and enduring definition of academic autonomy. The creation of professorial faculty boards under the reign of Leopold II was short lived mainly due to the fear that a greater degree of self-government would lead to the universities espousing the detestable doctrines of the French revolution.

Nevertheless, the harnessing of the university to the process of modernization did have implications for the issue of academic autonomy and, more particularly, the delicate and perennial question of how to balance the independence that scholarship requires against the rights of the state to have some measure of control over law, theology and medicine. In 1798, Emmanual Kant set out a model of autonomy which recognized the right of the state to intervene in those areas which directly influenced the well-being and thinking of its citizens (Reiss 1987). Such intervention, he argued, did not apply to philosophy for a number of reasons. First, because philosophy was concerned with scholarship and truth rather than with the administration of public order; second, because it had to be free from external constraints if it were to judge the teaching of other faculties; and third, because Man is by nature free and under no constraint save that involved in the pursuit of truth. On all three grounds, therefore, state regulation in the area of philosophy was inappropriate. The Kantian model of academic autonomy rested on a fundamental dualism between those activities where the state might intervene and those where it might not. As we shall see later, the dualism of Kant's model is of more than passing relevance to the situation as it has evolved over the past fifteen years or so in Western Europe.

While Kant acknowledged the legitimacy of state authority in certain specific fields, von Humboldt interpreted the role of the state in a minimalist fashion. Its task was to ensure that the external conditions were appropriate for the maintenance of 'freedom to teach and to learn' (*Lern – und – Lehrfreiheit*):

> The State should see only to the wealth (i.e. the strength and variety) of intellectual vigour by choosing the men to be assembled and guarantee the freedom of their work . . . the main thing is the choice of the men to be set to work . . . Next to that, a small number of organisational laws which should be simple but have a profound effect, is of prime importance.
>
> (Humboldt, quoted in Berchem 1985, p. 246)

Von Humboldt's concept of academic autonomy differed in several ways from that of Kant. In the first place, he did not regard the existence of the state as conflicting with the 'inner life' of academe. On the contrary, one of the essential expressions of statehood was a common cultural identity. One of its prime functions was the advancement of culture, learning and teaching, for the well-being of science and in particular those disciplines that 'generated reason' (Kunzel 1982, p.244). Furthermore, as the patron of culture and science, a central element in the state's mission *vis-à-vis* the university was the protection of disinterested science against sectarian pressures from within and from without academe. In von Humboldt's notion of academic freedom, the state itself served as a 'buffer organ' against outside pressures, not least of which was the utilitarianism associated with the 'rising industrial classes'. That the state underwrote the university's commitment 'only to the interests of science and learning' (Mullinger 1911, p. 767) involved it in a species of self-denying ordinance in those matters associated with research and teaching. This is not to say, however, that the university was not accountable, in its turn, to public authority. As the major instrument for the training of the administrative and educational élite, it was answerable to Ministries of Education. Lines of administrative accountability were clearly drawn and given physical expression in the person of the curator, a civil servant with ultimate responsibility for administrative and economic issues.

In place of the Kantian duality, where intervention was legitimate in 'vocational areas' while preserving an 'autonomous domain' for philosophy, the Humboldtian model redefined this duality in the form of a descending administrative hierarchy – the lines of accountability to the Ministry – and an ascending academic hierarchy which reposed on an individual interpretation of the freedom to teach and to learn. For, although von Humboldt sought to bring together both student and teacher as part of an organic community of scholarship, this community was not a community of equals. Rather it incorporated various degrees of individual autonomy with the highest, and thus freest, expression being found in the individual full chairholder, around whom were grouped co-workers, assistants, students and aspirants, forming part of a 'school of thought'. Thus, in contrast to Britain and the United States, the concept of academic autonomy did not assume a collegial form across all grades. Autonomy was, then, individual not institutional.

A third model of the relationship between government and higher education is found in the Napoleonic university. And, just as the Humboldtian model provided the basis for the development of higher education systems in Austria, Norway, Sweden and Denmark, the Napoleonic model provided the template for universities in Italy, Spain and certain Latin American countries such as Chile and Brazil. If the Humboldtian interpretation of academic autonomy rested on a species of partnership in which the state provided the legislative framework within which the university advanced culture and learning, and thus afforded a higher expression of the state as a cultural entity, the Napoleonic model rested on a clear subordination of the university to the state. The university's mission was to ensure the political stability and unity of the nation in a physical sense. This stood in contrast to the Humboldtian interpretation in which culture, science or learning existed over and above the state. In their particular ways, both models corresponded to a particular interpretation of nationalism, but with this difference: in Humboldt's Prussia cultural unity was not coterminous with the state, but went beyond into other German-speaking areas of middle Europe. In France, the revolutionary doctrine of the Republic, one and indivisible, brought both state and nation together by administrative means. Teaching and learning were not conceived as independent of the state, but rather as expressions of a unity that had already been achieved.

Teaching and learning were thus subject to legislative oversight by central government acting as the incarnation of the nation, its culture, ambition and genius. Nowadays, our views of highly centralized systems of university administration cause us to forget how revolutionary this model was and some of the positive aspects that underlay it. In the first place, formal bureaucratic control by central administration over such matters as selection and appointment to tenured posts is a means of upholding universalistic criteria for judging merit and advancement. The state acts as the ultimate guarantor against corporate reproduction (CRE Information 1983, pp. 87–95). In the second place, it served to maintain the quality and institutional homogeneity in the university sector and, in the third place, it was conceived as a means of upholding national unity by ensuring the formal equality of provision and services, programmes and courses amongst universities. (Neave and Rhoades 1987, *op. cit.*, p. 224).

Though some scholars see the Napoleonic university as operating drastic changes in the concept of academic self governance (Carreras 1987, pp. 31–32), this too has to be placed in context. Certainly, the designation of university teachers as one of a series of technical arms of central government (as a corps universitaire) did major violence to hitherto held notions of corporate autonomy. But this was little more than extending to the university world the abolition of corporate and guild privileges enacted earlier in 1792 by the Le Chapellier law. More important, however, was the effect of this incorporation upon the way in which autonomy was conceived and, until the late 1960s, continued to be conceived. Autonomy was not regarded as being coterminous with the pursuit of scholarship and with the maintenance of particular privilege, of serving vested, sectoral and self interest, rather than of service to the nation. The Napoleonic model did not permit the inclusion of academic autonomy as part of the legitimate relationship between government and university, since to have done so would have been to deny the universal nature of the writ of government. Far from being a species of 'reserved area' contained within a general legislative frame, which distinguished the Humboldtian theory, institutional autonomy in France was less a matter of formal theory than a series of marginal activities over which the state had not seen fit explicitly to extend its purlieu. An alternative view of autonomy as manifest in the Napoleonic model would be to see it as residing in the *initiation* of procedures which ultimately required official sanction – for example promotion and the development of new national degree courses.

A fourth model of autonomy is that found in Britain. The basis on which the British theory of academic autonomy rests is one derived from Whig constitutional theory of the eighteenth century, reinforced by nineteenth century Liberal theories of the State. In contrast to either France or Germany, Britain saw no general attack on the corporate stance of academia. In short, as with many of our social institutions, the political revolution which took place in Continental Europe in the latter part of the eighteenth and early nineteenth century had no counterpart here. Thus the university was neither incorporated as part of the national bureaucracy, nor was it subject to any one coherent constitutional or administrative theory of the relationship between state and university. The status of academia as a property-owning corporation of scholars, the purest expression of which was in the two ancient English universities, was preserved. And, though other models grew up with the rise of the provincial universities, these have gradually assumed extensive self-government and internal self-validation (Eustace 1982). It is, of course, not coincidental that the corporation of scholars should have retained its importance in Britain. There are at least two reasons for this. First, because until the First World War, British political life had no concept of 'the State' as a distributive or regulative entity. Second, and more particularly in the field of education, there existed a broadly held view which regarded education, and cultural responsibilities by extension, as ill-served by state intervention (Simon 1964). In other words, the British model of academic autonomy derived not from the action of the state defining a 'reserve area' of non-intervention but rather from the absence of a concept of the role of the state which itself could serve to legitimize such a definition. Hence, there could be no concept corresponding to the Humboldtian arrangement by which the state itself served as a buffer to ensure commitment to scholarship and learning. Such commitment was self-regulated by the non-written practices of academia. Nor, for the same reason, could there be an acceptable theory, within the confines of Liberal constitutionalism, of the state setting down the 'external limits' to academic autonomy, for the simple reason that such an act would have involved some measure of intervention.

Nevertheless, there was an aspect of autonomy which the British model held in common with Humboldt. This was the idea of the 'facilitatory state'. Under this interpretation, the state's role was to provide the financial means. In this, the setting up of the University Grants Committee (UGC) in 1919 marked a crucial point in the accumulation of practice which, hardened into accepted convention, formed the bedrock on which academic autonomy reposed in the United Kingdom. Though some observers have seen the creation of the UGC as a means of arming the university against the pressing demands of industry (Scott 1984) (itself an interesting parallel to some of the reasons Humboldt advanced for the stae underwriting autonomy), it did not give rise to autonomy as a 'reserved area'. Rather it created an area of negotiation between state and university which was, in effect, controlled by the universities themselves. Exaggerated though this view might be, the foundation of the UGC is a mirror image of the Napoleonic University. For while the latter penetrated deeply into academe, so the former penetrated deeply into central government. And, in contradistinction to the Humboldtian theory of autonomy, it did not cast the state as 'buffer'. Rather it set up a buffer which was itself an extension of the university.

Two features set aside the British notion of academic autonomy from the models that have gone before. First, unlike either France or Germany, autonomy was *individual* and *institutional*, both of which were based on the individual Charter and the collegial style of self-government (Becher and Kogan 1980). Second, while Charters secured in principle institutional autonomy, the 'zone of negotiation' between universities and government was not based on any detailed code of regulation. It rested on 'the establishment and maintenance of trust and confidence' between the two parties (Templeman 1982, p. 25).

Such a relationship was, perhaps, one of the more interesting examples of that flexibility which is commonly held to be one of the advantages of an unwritten constitution and, so long as mutual 'trust and confidence' reigned, it went far in conferring upon the British university system an adaptability to growth and change which others, burdened by the formalities of administrative procedure, noted and some imitated. But, by the same token, in the absence of any formal administrative or constitutional definition of academic autonomy, there existed no way of defending established procedures in the 'zone of negotiation' should government, like Shaw's gentleman, decide to change the rules of the game. That said, if I were to take a European view on the British model of autonomy, I would be inclined to say that the outstanding characteristic of the British model is surely that it survived for so long on the basis of unspoken convention, understanding and agreements reached within the 'zone of negotiation'. A second feature, which follows from this, would appear to be that the 'zone of negotiation' was itself an extension into central government of that style of collegiality and relative informality which existed at the level of the individual establishment (Becher *et al.* 1977).

Forces of change

If I have been overlong in exploring models of autonomy in certain western European countries, this is because they provided the basic framework within which higher education moved towards mass status. In continental Europe, though not in Britain, the expansion of higher education contributed powerfully to redefining the nature of academic autonomy. From the latter part of the 1960s established models, the origins of which could be traced back over the previous century and a half, were revised often in great haste. From that moment on – and the moment obviously varied from country to country – the idea of autonomy took on an instability and a political centrality that it had not had this century. If one were to sum up the general thrust of the various policies that emerged from the upheavals from May 1968 onwards, they entailed redrawing the boundary between the university and the state.

Some may disagree with the idea of replacing the concept of academic autonomy with that of boundary. But there are several reasons why this change in analogue is more satisfactory. The most relevant of these is that autonomy carries with it certain overtones which stress *continuity* in the relationship between university and state. It implies a certain enduring consensus as to those areas in which the state, as we have seen in the Humboldtian model, chose not to intervene. It also carries with it a certain fixity. Yet, to any observer of higher education over the past two decades in western Europe, it is precisely the break with previous practice that stands out. In place of consensus has emerged a situation of conflict over the part that the university ought to play in society – between 'socially' or 'economically' relevant or 'economically necessary' fields of study – or, as part of the internal redefinition of management and governance, over who should participate in the affairs of the university. Furthermore, the concept of boundary is dynamic. It undergoes considerable shifts, sometimes in the direction of closer external oversight by government, sometimes in the sense of enhanced internal participation. It is clear, for example, that the current thrust of reform in the United Kingdom is to shift the boundary or frontier of control in favour of central authority. On the other hand, the French 1968 *Loi d'Orientation* recognized officially and for the first time that universities had autonomy to the extent that it involved control over teaching, staff–student participation in areas of common interest and the right to develop inter-disciplinary studies (Leroy 1982). In terms of our boundary analogy, the 1968 Law in France extended the boundary of autonomy to the benefit of the university (Neave 1982).

The question that lies behind 'autonomy as boundary' is: what were the forces that brought about change? It would be tempting to say that in Britain, as in many western European countries, this was due to a political revision in the role and mission of higher education. But in the British case there is sufficient evidence to suggest that the major factor was short-term, pragmatic and financial (Kogan 1984). What is seen as diminishing institutional autonomy in this country is more in the nature of an add-on or an elaboration of a policy the *raison d'être* of which was primarily economic. Such was not the situation in France, the Federal Republic of Germany or the Netherlands, where the central issue from May 1968 onwards took academic autonomy as its focus.

Complex and often confusing though the movement for participation in university affairs was, it can be reduced to several themes. The first of these –

and particularly developed in France and Italy – was the rediscovery by certain student groups of the Bologna model of autonomy. That is, the autonomy of students to learn and to have some measure of control over those who teach. A second strand which grew out of this and received much airing in France before Edgar Faure culled up his *Loi d'Orientation*, was the idea of cutting universities free from central administration and conferring on them powers to organize outside the purlieu of the Ministry of Education. What started as a challenge to the individual autonomy of academic staff moved over to the rather broader issue of institutional autonomy. Should higher education be organized entirely independently of the state?

This latter proposal was not entertained for long (Chalendar 1970) though it showed clearly the degree of dissatisfaction present. Demands for autonomy did not, however, fall on deaf ears. The *Loi d'Orientation* acknowledged the principle of autonomy at institutional level, though an autonomy by no means as wide-ranging as many would have wished. By so doing it put an end to the Napoleonic concept of university and, by the same stroke of the pen, placed the model of university–government relationship in France firmly on the concept of a 'reserved area' in which a measure of institutional self-management was located.

In those countries where higher education had been influenced by the German model of university, the push to redefine autonomy concentrated on the internal balance of power between students, junior staff and chairholders rather than on the external linkage between university and government. The bone of contention lay in what was termed earlier the 'degrees of individual auton-omy' which coalesced around the full professor. Rather than challenging the principle of autonomy, representatives of non-professorial staff sought to *extend* it to those hitherto excluded – in short, to replace the University of the Professors (*Ordinarienuniversität*) by a university of group decision-making (*Gruppenuniversität*) with rights of representation on the main organs of internal management.

The response of governments to these remonstrances brought forth a spate of legislation in Austria, Denmark, the Netherlands and the Federal Republic of Germany, most of which acknowledged the basic claims for group representa-tion and participation: the Danish Parliamentary Act of 1973, the Austrian University Organization Law of 1975, the Dutch *Wet op de Universitaire Bestuur-leiding* of the previous year and the German *Hochschulrahmengesetz* that followed in 1976. From the limited perspective of internal autonomy, the common feature of these enactments was to lay down certain principles for the representation of group interests. In some cases, as in Austria, the Netherlands and the Federal Republic of Germany, this took the form of a tripartite arrangement (*Drittelpar-ität*) in which all three constituences – students, professorial and non-professorial staff – had equal representation. Whether these measures were an extension of autonomy or, as has been argued by certain senior scholars, its curtailment (Shils and Daalder 1982, Chapman 1983) is, like as not, a matter of where one sits in the ranks of academe. What is a professor's fragmentation and demagogy is doubtless an assistant's revival of 'true' autonomy, and a restatement of that organic community between student and teachers that von Humboldt originally envisaged.

Whatever one's view on the matter, the burden of legislation was to give a broader definition of who might participate in the internal affairs of the university. However, the process of defining structures and responsibilities to accommodate pressures inside academe also led to legislation of a more general sort which set down the overall administrative and legal framework within which university systems functioned. Regardless of the exact terms used – University Guideline Law in France, Higher Education Framework Law in the Federal Republic of Germany, the Danish Act dealing with 'The Administration of Institutions of Higher Education' or the Austrian University Organization Law – all involved the state in redefining the boundary of external control. In Denmark, for example, though universities were recognized as self-governing institutes, increased emphasis was placed on 'coordination between Ministry and individual establishments (Neave 1987). In Austria, if the Higher Education Organization Act acknowledged the basis of internal power-sharing, it reaffirmed the principle of higher education being legally and financially under the direct control of the state (Neave 1986).

The more usual interpretation of this legislative orgy of the mid-1970s in western Europe sees it as a response to student unrest, and as I have suggested, creating an 'autonomous reserve' within the legislative framework (Kamp 1986). In parallel to settling the internal affairs of academe, governments were also committed to revising the mechanisms of co-ordination to accommodate the new reality – administrative, managerial and financial – of higher education systems rapidly assuming all the complexities of mass status. In his analysis of those forces involved in co-ordinating higher education, Clark drew up a three-dimensional typology based on the relative weight of the market, academic oligarchy and the state (Clark 1983). If the events of the late 1960s and early 1970s are analysed in Clark's terms, it is clear that, just as the State stepped in to recognize – though perhaps temporarily – a waning in the forces of oligarchy inside the academic estate, so it also strengthened its formal powers of co-ordination within the external frame. Thus, the emergence of new decision-making units below the Faculty level – whether the French *Unité d'Enseignement de Recherche*, the Dutch *Vakgroep* or the German *Fachbereich*, symbolic of the new model of academic autonomy based on the principle of power sharing – was offset by a thickening of the external administrative overlay.

Strengthening the administrative overlay

Many students of comparative higher education have remarked on the increasing tendency of governments to intervene directly and more actively in the affairs of higher education, more particularly so from the mid-1970s onward. The reasons for this more active stance are several: to regulate student admissions in certain key areas, engineering and medicine being the most obvious, where demand rapidly outstripped supply; to create new budgetary criteria, often involving the separation of student numbers as the main criteria of allocation and, more recently, to profile the type of research that public authorities feel universities ought to undertake. The tale is one familiar to most western European countries over the past half decade or so. There are, however, a number of different processes as well as different perception of how the university should function that lie beneath this general trend. The first of these is an increase in what may be termed the 'depth of penetration' of public policy into the fabric of academe.

If one takes a global view of developments over the past decade in the universities of western Europe, the one outstanding development is the change in the nature of government intervention. This has altered radically from relatively routine adjustments to admissions policy and the overhaul of the structure of doctoral level studies in France (OECD 1986, *Conseil Supérieur de la Recherche et de la Technologie* 1986), to the restructuring of graduate studies in the Netherlands (Bijleveld 1987) as well as major efforts either to expand the research base as in France and Sweden, or to shift the emphasis towards science, technology, computer-based development and biotechnology, which are matters of universal preoccupation. The details and the particular variations between different countries are interesting, but not of themselves especially illuminating. What they illustrate, however, is a fundamental displacement of the boundary of government control into areas which earlier fell into what I have termed the 'zone of negotiation'.

If this trend is, to all intents and purposes, universal at the present time, it began to gather force in western Europe from around 1981 onwards. However, in Europe, by contrast with Britain, it is possible to see certain elements of continuity which carried over from the mid-1970s' Concordat between government and higher education on the matter of internal power-sharing. The most important of these was the move to enhanced 'community participation' in university affairs. Just as the Concordat set up a new system of internal governance, so certain governments sought to bring in the external world to act as a species of check and balance. Though the timing differs, beginning for example in 1977 in Sweden and the Federal Republic and forming a significant element in the Spanish Law of University Reform of 1983 and, predictably, a point of high controversy in the 1984 *Loi d'Orientation* in France, the drive towards multiplying the external constituencies at local and regional level forms an important aspect in the strengthening of the administrative overlay (Premfors 1984, Kluge 1984, Carreras 1987, Pedro 1988, Neave 1985). The formal purpose behind such developments was to tighten up the linkage between university and region, to give the latter some say in the development of curricula to meet regional skill needs and, in the case of the German Study Commissions, to give a new fluidity to the process of innovation. In the case of Spain, the powers granted to the 'Autonomous Communities' were even more far-reaching. In addition to having financial powers – a characteristic also shared by the Swedish Regional Committees – Spanish regional governments also have the power to define the nature of university autonomy itself as well as the various structures to underpin it. (Pedro, *op. cit.*)

Now, if academic autonomy is in essence, the right of staff in higher education to determine the nature of their work, then the advent of bodies such as these may not, of itself, restrict that right. They do, however, increase the number of stakeholders as well as giving further weight to the view that the university is a *public* service rather than a community of scholars. And this, in turn, brings about a subtle alteration in the public perception of academic autonomy. It is, in short, defined in terms of visible public service that is external and sustained to the extent that academia is willing to perform those public services as laid down by external agencies. On the other hand, such a public definition tends to discount the 'private' definition of academic autonomy held by many of those inside higher education which is the pursuit and development of particular disciplines, not all of which may readily correspond to the basic utilitarianism implied in the former. The private definition is then acceptable only insofar as it falls in with the public one. The extension of the publc overlay which, I am suggesting, began from bottom up over the period 1977 to 1984, was not simply that it added a further layer to the process of negotiating change. It also constituted an important step in the overall process which most of our systems of higher education see today – namely, the external redefinition not only of the stakeholders whose influence bears down on deciding priorities in academic work, but a redefinition of what is considered 'legitimate' academic autonomy. The danger in this redefinition lies not in the apparent conflict between public utilitarianism and private disciplinary identity and values so much as in the very real possibility that defence of the private concept of autonomy is seen negatively as the simple restatement of corporative self-interest – a view which I suggested earlier accompanied the rise of that most centralized of models, the Napoleonic university.

The extension of the administrative overlay was not confined to the regional level. More recently, it has begun to emerge at the national level as well. Though it would be wrong to see these as two deliberately complementary processes, nevertheless they have this effect. This second process is associated with the rise of what Trow has termed 'instruments of public purpose' – essentially bodies under the ambit of the appropriate Ministry but endowed with a specific responsibility for controlling particular aspects or sectors of the nation's higher education system: student numbers, resource distribution and/or monitoring, performance evaluation (Trow 1980). Some of these grew out of bodies which previously underpinned the 'zone of negotiation' between university and government and it is here that Britain joins in a common European development with the very rapid alteration in function of the UGC over the period from 1981. Others, such as the French *Comité National d'Evaluation* or the Spanish *Consejo de Universidades*, set up in 1983, or the enhanced powers of the Dutch National Inspectorate over the university sector, have been created to give added focus to the co-ordination and evaluation of higher education at the systems level and at the level of individual establishments (Staropouli 1987, ICED 1987, NRC Handelsblad 1985).

The significance of these bodies is, to a very large extent, moulded by the particular context in which they are located. And if they are designed to give better purchase to public authorities and emerge as a manifestation of what may be called the 'Evaluative State', their relationship to the concept of autonomy is very different. In the case of both France and Spain, the strengthening of co-ordination and evaluation is seen as necessary *because* the legislator is bent on increasing the degree of institutional autonomy provided for in the 1984 French *Loi d'Orientation* and the 1983 Spanish Law on University Reform. A similar argument accompanied the Dutch reforms (Ministerie van Onderwijs en Wetenschappen 1985). In systems such as those just mentioned, which have been subject to highly detailed and centralized control, the additional strategic oversight implied in these bodies may be seen as a positive trade-off against a greater margin of initiative at the level of institutional autonomy. It is the lesser of two evils. The same enhanced strategic oversight implied in the new arrangements for the Universities Funding Council (UFC) in Britain may have a certain parallelism. But in a system in which institutional autonomy appeared in the recent past to be well nigh total there can surely be no trade-off because any increase in central control *must* be a diminution in the degree of autonomy; not granted for that would imply recognition of legitimate state power so to do, but evolved through the growth of higher education itself. Thus the manner in which similar policy thrusts are received is largely determined by the prevalent institutional practices and values in which they are inserted.

Re-definition of autonomy

The expansion in the number of external constituencies at regional level and the subsequent growth of 'instruments of public purpose' raises the question: 'In what way was the concept of university autonomy altered?' Some clues to the answer lie in the basic purpose behind each of these developments. Regionalization, I have suggested, was a form of external rebalancing to enhanced internal participation. It opened a further dimension of public service for which both university and region could negotiate the terms. It was, in short, another option that, in the minds of several governments, the French and the Swedish for example, the university could pursue. Yet 'instruments of public purpose' acting at the national level were not only evaluative instruments. They were also means by which governments could ascertain how far universities had conformed to stated national priorities. Certainly their very presence illustrates the fact that in European higher education systems, whether the aim is to attenuate the internal forces of oligarchy, to rebalance those of co-ordination or to bring system and labour market into closer links, all three forces are mediated by central government. In the British case, obviously, the first two do not pertain. But Jarratt and to some extent Croham too, are significant moves towards the third.

With the arrival of these bodies – and it is correct in my opinion to see the latter day UGC as part of them and the Universities Funding Council as well as the Polytechnics and Colleges Funding Council (PCFC) in the same light – the type of 'public service' that the universities were expected to perform was no longer subject to negotiation. It had been set down in government statements of priority. The main issue under question was whether the individual university was on the way to fulfilling, or had fulfilled, the targets or priorities, whether expressed in student subject balance, graduation rates, staff–student ratios etc, that had been set down by the appropriate Ministry. This, in short, was an obligatory definition of 'public service' in contrast to the often permissive definition laid down with regard to 'public service' to the region. Both dimensions involved a concept of public service or commitment to the external community. In the case of national priorities, it was non-negotiable. Indeed, the purpose of instruments of public purpose was to provide that intelligence which would permit central administration to reward the performing and to chastise the laggardly.

The consequences of this are two-fold. First, the main task of the university is being redefined in terms of commitment to one predominant sector of the national community, viz. industry and national productivity. Second, autonomy is now itself negotiable either on a yearly basis or, depending on the time-scale of strategic planning, on a three-yearly basis. Autonomy, or that degree of self-governance that the various systems of higher education in say, France, the Netherlands and Britain have enjoyed is now 'conditional'.

'Conditional autonomy' is a highly significant revision and is as central to understanding the way present day relations between government and higher education are evolving as the four theoretical models outlined in the earlier part of this essay. It merits closer examination. Britain is an interesting example of conditional autonomy if only for the fact that it has come about so rapidly, and also because the period between the late 1960s and the early 1980s was uncluttered with the complexities of redefining the nature of academic autonomy internally or in terms of regionalization. The British concept of autonomy rested, as I have said, on the notion of the 'facilitatory state', an agreement by which central government underwrote the financial needs of the university sector, leaving the issues of quality, maintenance, governance, degree validation, staff appointments – aspects which in other European countries required active ratification by central authority – in the hands of the individual establishment. What has happened since 1981 is a massive reversal in the purpose of the zone of negotiation. Instead of being an extension of the university into central government, it has become a 'zone of penetration' of central government into the university world, and a vehicle for setting an increasing number of norms whether in terms of subject viability, differential resource allocation, efficiency or the creation of internal cost/accountability structures. This proliferation of system norms over the past six years has, I would argue, exactly the same function as those legislative changes that took place in Europe in the period from 1968 onwards; namely, the creation of framework legislation, the purpose of which was to redefine internal autonomy and external system control the better to shape higher education to government intent. Seen from this perspective, the purpose of the French *Loi d'Orientation* of 1968 and the British Education Act two decades later are very similar. The formal difference is that the latter does not confine itself simply to questions of higher education. And, as doubtless those of a less charitable turn of mind will be quick to point out, the French in its hobble-kneed fashion sought to give some expression to the notion of internal autonomy. The British Framework Law is, on the contrary, rather economical with that same quality.

There are, to be sure, differences of detail between current British higher education policy and contemporary developments in France and the Netherlands. The tripartite stratification of universities for research purposes put about by the Advisory Body for the Research Councils stands in marked contrast with French policy which, since 1981, has involved expanding the research base across the university sector and the Grandes Ecoles (*Le Monde-Campus* 1987). The closure of smaller and 'less viable' departments in Britain can be seen in the same light as the task-concentration and distribution exercise carried out in the Netherlands from 1983 onwards (Ministerie van Onderwijs en Wetenschappen 1983). Despite these differences, there is nevertheless a clear overall trend. It is towards externalizing those functions that lie at the heart of academic autonomy – peer review, self evaluation, corporate judgement by peers of the quality of the work inside the various disciplinary cultures that go to make up academe – and relocating them as countervailing instruments of external oversight in central administration. And often in the hands of a state clerisy whose essential dilemma must constantly and for ever remain whether their judgement is to be exercised within the canons of their one-time discipline or to conform to the will of the Prince.

The redefinition of autonomy as 'conditional autonomy' is not a direct attack on the conditions by which internal autonomy at institutional level is exercised, though to this there is perhaps one exception in Britain, namely the vexed issue of revision in the terms of tenure. Its effects are, rather, indirect. Autonomy can be exercised only *on condition* that the individual institute or department fulfils national or establishment norms which are continually to be renegotiated in the light of public policy. Thus, it is possible for both the British and the Netherlands governments to argue that reinforcement of the controlling framework is not directly antithetical to the exercise of autonomy. Any restriction introduced by individual establishments in response to changed external conditions is, after all, a decision reached by academics *en toute connaissance de cause*.

Conditional autonomy accentuates into a theory of academic behaviour those empirical developments which were touched upon earlier in connection with that phenomenon which I have called the 'thickening of the administrative overlay'. Accompanying this development is a dual concept of academic autonomy, identified as the public and the private interpretation of the same. Essentially our discussion arises from the differences between them, the second being argued by those inside academia, the former by public authorities. It is important to go a little deeper into the ideological grounding of the former since it is part of a wider social dynamic which, engineered or not, has evacuated a great deal of 'legitimacy' from historically based arguments in favour of 'autonomy'.

Central to the public interpretation of autonomy is the belief that the private interpretation – that of academics to shape and determine their own work – is antithetical to the competitive distribution of resources; that academia is judge and jury in its own case and that what passes for quality judgements are little more than clientelistic exchanges of favours, the purpose of which is to preserve a corporate control (whether disciplinary or institutional) over existing resources rather than seeking to distribute them where they will do the most good for the nation. Peer reviews, assessment and evaluation (according to this ideology, are not valid instruments for determining excellence or merit precisely because they are exercised inside the academic estate. To parody de Mandeville's *Fable of the Bees*, 'private competition is public incompetence.' Placed in this ideological setting, the goal of 'conditional' autonomy is to shift over the conditions governing competition from those defined according to the internal norms of academia to the external norms of what Max Beloff unkindly called Treasury clerks and accountants, in essence to increase the public visibility of the process of competition.

By the logic of the public interpretation, the process of review evaluation is brought out into the public arena and, as I argued earlier, placed in the hands of organizations, research councils or special review bodies which, once the main arenas in which excellence – the 'special coin of (academic) exchange' (Clark 1984, p. 270) – was evaluated by academia, now rest firmly as levers to enforce the public interpretation. Thus it is clear that the public concept of autonomy involves a major displacement of function and power in those bodies which, in happier times, were both symbolic and real expressions of academic service to the nation. Or, to revert to the analogue of 'boundary', such bodies, from being on the university side of the hedge, have now – to use an Americanism – 'gone over the hill'.

Conclusion

In this essay, I have sought to provide a perspective on the issue of academic autonomy which is both historical and comparative. My purpose in so doing was to show that autonomy, however much it may be presented in public dialogue, is not a whole. There are numerous interpretations of what is understood by this term, both across countries and across time. Today, just as yesterday, autonomy is not defined by academia. In most western European countries, it is defined by government, sometimes with the added protection of administrative law, sometimes by incorporating the right of 'freedom to teach and to learn' as part of the basic rights enshrined in a country's Constitution. The former arrangement is found in France, the latter in the Federal Republic of Germany, for example. Autonomy exists as a state of tension between various interests, between those of the external community and those of the academic community, between knowledge as an element in production and knowledge as an element of exploration. At certain times, the state has defined its role liberally in the sense of providing those conditions where university allegiance is held to be to scholarship and learning. This, I have suggested, was the idealistic model developed by von Humboldt. At other times, and most markedly so from the late 1960s onward, the state has stepped in to give a new entitlement to share in the benefits and responsibilities of internal self-management to new groups, At the present time, higher education faces the fact of a highly interventionary state, and none so marked as in the United Kingdom. If the drive towards what I have termed 'conditional autonomy' is a general characteristic underlying the changing relationship between university and polity in France, the Netherlands and the United Kingdom, the startling feature of this development is how quickly it grew in the latter country. Perhaps the situation reflects the fact that there were few constitutional devices to prevent it, since the entente between state and university reposed on the observance of unwritten practice and the observance of unwritten convention.

This is being changed. The 1988 Education Reform Act provides the framework legislation across all higher education sectors. What remains to be seen is to what degree academic autonomy in Britain will continue to be cast as a 'reserve domain' and what the final extent of its real territory will be.

5

Four Forms of Heresy in Higher Education: Aspects of Academic Freedom in Education for the Professions

Sinclair Goodlad

Freedom in any absolute sense is a chimera. We are all members one of another, locked into a creative interdependency. In discussing academic freedom, the need is to establish what freedom is desirable for whom and for what purpose. All freedom is ultimately based upon trust. For this reason, although academic freedom may appear primarily as a political issue, it is fundamentally a moral one involving our view concerning persons. The key issue is *how to maximize trust in persons* – seen not as isolated individuals but as responsible people willingly co-operating with one another.

To limit the field of enquiry, this chapter concentrates on some aspects of academic freedom in curriculum and pedagogy in education for the professions.

Within higher education, at least four kinds of freedom may be distinguished:

(a) the freedom of students to study at all: an issue concerning access;
(b) the freedom of students in what they learn and how they learn it: an issue concerning curriculum and pedagogy where the differences are between high levels of independence in learning contrasted with very closely controlled curricula;
(c) the freedom of faculty (members of the lecturing staff) to decide what to teach and how: issues concerning course approval, validation, and accreditation (Brubacher 1978, 55f);
(d) the freedom of faculty to carry out researches: an issue concerning choices to be made both by faculty themselves and by those who fund their researches on the relative intellectual, practical, financial and other merits of the claims of different programmes and projects for time and attention.

In each of the above cases, there are boundaries between, on the one hand, administratively and financially determined constraints, and, on the other hand, constraints deliberately imposed as political or other interference. The different types of freedom are in conflict with one another, and the conflicts are subject to

Figure 5.1

	Students		Faculty	
	Freedom to study	*Freedom to learn*	*Freedom to teach*	*Freedom to research*
Basic Unit	A	B	C	D
Institution	E	F	G	H
Profession	I	J	K	L
Sub-system	M	N	O	P
System	Q	R	S	T

continual and continuous modification politically at each point in our arrangements for higher education – what we cheerfully, but perhaps inaccurately, call the higher education *system*.

At each level of the system – from what Becher and Kogan (1980) call 'basic units', through institutions and professional accreditation bodies to the government-appointed committees controlling funding – there are restrictions on the freedoms of students and faculty (see Figure 5.1). A few examples of types of restriction will illustrate the types of conflict of interest that can occur.

Within basic units, there is a potential conflict between 'A', the freedom of students to study at all, and 'D', the freedom of faculty to devote time to their researches. Departments may be under pressure to select students of relatively homogeneous ability to diminish the hassle of planning teaching for a wide spread of ability and previous achievement, the object being to reduce the amount of time and attention paid to teaching and free as much time as possible for the researches of the faculty.

Again, the freedom of a profession, 'K', to decide what an intending professional should be required to know can be in conflict with the freedom of institutions, 'G', to decide what to teach. At system level, pressure from government for a widening of access, 'Q', can lead to an implicit reduction in the unit of resource so that departments, 'C', may not be able to afford teaching methods (such as field trips) which faculty believe necessary to maintain high quality in provision.

Conflicts of this sort are endemic in *any* arrangements for higher education, whatever their source of funding – public or private. What we need to ensure is that the administrative structures do the least possible damage to the activity they exist to sustain and develop. To this end it will be part of the argument of this paper that academic freedom is best nourished if responsibility for what is to be learned and how it is to be learned is pushed back as far down the line from system to individual as possible.

Much of the heat in the current debate in the United Kingdom (for example, concerning the 1988 Education Reform Bill) stems from the (correct) perception that a reduction of government funding for any or all of the methods by which the system is sustained is not only political (in the party sense) but also ideological in reflecting technical judgements (about both, for example, the relationships between economic inputs, such as research funding, and outputs, such as industrial competitiveness) and views concerning persons. Fascinating and urgent though the political issues are, it is the thesis of this paper that the debate must begin and end with moral issues, because the debate about freedom, including academic freedom, is ultimately about relationships between persons.

In that the basic arguments about academic freedom are moral ones, it must first be admitted that there are no *logical* determinants of which are right and which are wrong. Alasdair MacIntyre, for example, has argued at length (1981, 1985), that one cannot in fact make rational comment on the premises of moral systems: one must either accept or reject them. Commenting, for example, on two major competing systems, that of Rawls (1972) and that of Nozick (1974), he writes:

> Why should I accept Nozick's premises? He furnishes me with no reasons, but with a promissory note. Why should I accept Rawls's premises? They are, so he argues, those that would be accepted by hypothetical rational beings whose ignorance of their position in any social hierarchy enables them to plan a type of social order in which the liberty of each is maximized, in which inequalities are tolerated only insofar as they have the effect of improving the lot of the least well-off, and in which the good of liberty has priority over that of equality. But why should I in my actual social conditions choose to accept what those hypothetical rational beings would choose, rather than for example Nozick's premises about natural rights? And why should I accept what Rawls says about the priority of liberty over equality?
>
> (MacIntyre 1981:22)

Is, then, any system as good as any other? Obviously, not. But one is left with the dilemma of how to propound a view of persons, a theory of education and a justification for specific types of academic freedom which can command active assent. The approach adopted in this paper is to *assert* a position rather than to argue it, and to delineate it primarily by sketching some of the resistances and preferences it gives rise to. For this reason, and to sharpen focus on the position as much as possible, positions which deviate from it are called 'heresies' – a heresy being an exaggeration or corruption of 'the truth' in one direction or another. At the root of the argument is a view about the nourishment of persons as being the fundamental purpose of education. The concept of persons is, of course, contested (Peacocke and Gillett 1987). It is therefore necessary to begin with some sort of position statement concerning the nourishment of persons.

The moral position illustrated in what follows will seem crass when stated in bald, general terms: its value is in constituting a kind of 'situation ethic' which takes its life in concrete and specific contexts. Its roots are in Christian tradition, filtered through Enlightenment rationalism and existentialist criticism of rationalism; it is, in this sense, 'Christian-compatible' (to use Roy Niblett's phrase) rather than explicitly Christian.[1]

One can best delineate the position by means of Figure 5.2. The respect for

Figure 5.2

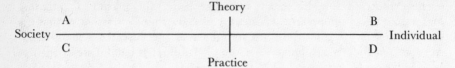

persons involved in this position seeks for each individual a balance between four preoccupations; and because we spend most of our lives in collaboration with one another through social institutions, the position seeks a similar balance in institutional arrangements within the limits of what is administratively and financially possible:

1 Theory (Ideas): In many ways, the distinguishing marks of being human are those concerned with the mind – the organizing power of intellect as revealed variously in works of art, scientific theories, political theories, and so forth.

2 Practice: Yet, obviously, although we do not live by bread alone, we do live by bread. 'Practice' refers to everything concerned with the basic apparatus of living. In this regard, the Theory/Practice axis echoes theological concepts of the Transcendent and the Mundane. The other axis, likewise, does not claim to be original: the dichotomy it represents is, for example, the substance of Tiryakian's *Sociologism and Existentialism* (1962).

3 Society: In an important sense, persons are aggregations of social roles; they cannot be described as definable entities except through language which locates the person as father, son, wife, daughter, factory-worker, citizen, etc. Becoming acquainted with the requirements of social roles of various degrees of complexity is a major part of individual learning; it is often the *raison d'être* of much education.

4 Individual: Yet, if we treat persons as a sort of fluid that flows, or is poured, into a set of predefined social roles, we deny the fundamental element (upon which most existentialist writers insist) of a person's capacity for choice. Individuality, even eccentricity, is fundamental – even if most of us most of the time conform to social expectations, our sense of what it is to be a person is constantly nourished by those who make unusual or individualistic statements (in writing, music, paint, stone, by climbing improbable peaks or sailing alone around the world, and so forth).

A society which, by accident or by design, systematically and irrecoverably limits persons' opportunities in any of these dimensions is at fault. 'The good life', in this perspective, is one in which persons are intellectually alert (stimulated by theories and ideas), with needs adequately provided for by the apparatus of social life (practice), responsive to and actively involved with the greatest possible range of institutions through which their society takes its life, and yet able to exercise sufficient choice to define themselves as individuals. When we speak of 'freedom', we probably have some such picture in mind.

Learning is the process by which persons establish their identity (intellectual, physical, social) within the matrix established by these axes; education is the social process by which this learning is given shape and direction. Education implies organization, purpose, institutions. In every aspect of higher education, (curriculum, teaching methods, research, collegial organization), choices have to be made of what can and should be done; specialization of function is an operational necessity. But the thesis of this paper is that if education, in *any* institutional form, neglects any one of the needs of persons indicated above, it is deficient.

Individuals may wish to become specialists in a particular area; however, educating *institutions* represent an act of collective will. While institutions undoubtedly need to specialize for reasons of technical efficiency, the position here sketched would require deliberate, systematic fidelity to the concept of a person to be expressed in institutional arrangements. If educational practice (in curriculum, teaching methods, research, or college organization) drifts off into any one of the quadrants (A, B, C, D of Figure 5.2), to the neglect of the other issues involved in concern for persons, some form of 'heresy' is in danger of being perpetrated.

To give some flesh and bones to these ideas, the following paragraphs will discuss some aspects of education for the professions. The approach will be articulated along the following dimensions: Issues, Heresies, and Preferences.

Issues

Curriculum theory

Many of the most interesting and important questions about the design of curricula in higher education can be located on the axes of Figure 5.2. A theory of knowledge is necessarily implied by the organizing ideas and concepts of disciplines. The personal philosophy of life of the individual can hardly help but be influenced by encounters with new ideas and information. Because curricula represent control of learning they necessarily involve society, in that those who devise curricula must be responsive (either by direct market forces or by more bureaucratic forms of accountability) to social agencies; the massive apparatus of accreditation, validation, and evaluation is abundant witness to this. Finally, curricula relate to practice if not by design, then by accident; even studies seemingly unrelated to the necessities of daily life (history, literature, philosophy, etc.) impart skills (such as those of careful reading, precise writing, the capacity to sift large quantities of information) which are fundamental in many forms of administration. Each of the four factors is important on its own; but it is above all the attempt to maintain a reasonable balance between them for any individual person (and, therefore, in the offerings of each individual educating institution) that makes education liberal. 'Heresies' which result from over-absorption with any one element are identified below.

In most academic disciplines, 'theory' constitutes a complex of ideas, internally consistent and rich in interconnections with other areas of inquiry, which gives perspective and order to a field of inquiry. As I have suggested elsewhere

(Goodlad and Pippard 1982:73), it is very often theory which distinguishes higher learning in its institutionalized forms from similar learning as undertaken by individuals. Compare, for example, a radio ham with an electrical engineer, an antiquary with an historian, a naturalist with a botanist, a journalist with a political scientist. In each of the pairs, the first person listed accumulates ideas and information but without the peer-pressure which an academic experiences to fit them into complex frameworks.

There is no reason at all why people should not accumulate whatever information they desire. However, the collective will implied by educating institutions indicates the need for some principle of selection, some method of ordering perception. Theory distinguishes academic studies from their culturally primary forms: e.g. cooking/nutrition, construction/engineering, worship/theology, literature/literary criticism, politics/political science, musical performance/musicology. The primary form is just as useful and desirable as (often, in fact, more useful and desirable in some ways than) its theoretical correlate. In higher education, institutional coherence often derives from a certain concentration of effort. Universities, for example, have concentrated on explanation, classification, analysis; other types of institution develop the primary cultural form directly (e.g. restaurants, factories, churches, theatres, parliament, orchestras) or as instruction for the exigencies of practice (e.g. hotel schools, technical colleges, theological seminaries, drama schools, political 'cells', conservatoires). For depth of understanding in any field of learning, however, it may well be necessary for a student of nutrition both to study biochemistry and to work in a kitchen, for an engineer both to study strength of materials and to work in a factory, for a theology student both to study biblical criticism and to work in a church, for a student of literature both to study literary criticism and to work in a publishing house, for a political science student both to study political theory and to work as a research assistant to a member of parliament, for a music student both to study musicology and to play an instrument.

The emphasis on practice can not only, perhaps, prevent academic theory from drifting off into meaninglessness or crankiness; in college curricula, it may be a psychological necessity for students. Practice alone is, of course, not enough; without some co-ordinating theory, some inter-connectedness of ideas, purely practical subjects can ossify or degenerate into a congeries of rules-of-thumb and obsession with technique. Practice without theory can become basely conservative; theory without practice can become arcane, unintelligible or simply trivial. The obvious practical implication of these remarks is that just as it may be desirable for students in institutions which emphasize theory (e.g. universities) to be exposed to practice, so it may be desirable for students in institutions which emphasize practice (trade or vocational schools) to be exposed to theory.

With structural unemployment becoming, it seems, a growing menace in many societies, it is no kindness to individuals at any level of education to leave them without skills with which to earn a living. But this does not imply transforming education into skills-training; rather it may involve the systematic analysis of the marketable skills which an individual acquires while pursuing studies which are not specifically related to work. Counselling and career-guidance may be necessary to prevent students feeling that they have to neglect the transcendent in pursuit of the mundane.

On the society–individual axis, the principal issue is that of autonomy and accountability. Individual persons need time and space in which to work out their personal philosophies of life. How, when, where is this to be provided? It is not enough for educating institutions to say that this is someone else's business (e.g. churches, political parties, families); some sort of facilitating activity is required in the curriculum offering students the opportunity (which not all, of course, may wish to take) to reflect on matters of ultimate concern. What makes life complicated is that the need or desire for opportunities for reflection occurs at different ages for different individuals, as William Perry (1970, 1981), for example, has shown.

The emphasis on society in the discussion of curricula recalls that academic disciplines are institutional phenomena, with all the apparatus of learned societies, peer assessment, journals, and so forth. Academic knowledge is consensus knowledge. In the formation of knowledge, the freedom of individual scholars to follow ideas wherever they lead has preserved the individual *vis-a-vis* society'. In the dissemination of knowledge through curricula, what nowadays preserves the academic freedom of educational institutions or of individual teachers and students within them? The thesis here advanced is that academic freedom, in the sense of reasonable freedom for manoeuvre for the faculty in teaching and in the sense of offering liberal education to students, resides in a balance being achieved between the concerns sketched in Figure 5.2.

Theory of learning

If curriculum is the process by which ideas become institutionalized, teaching methods are transactions by which curriculum is mediated to learners from teachers. In one sense, teaching methods only become important in situations of constraint – where people are required to learn things which by natural inclination they would not learn, or which other people require them to learn for some socially agreed purpose. Indeed, 'teaching' may in some instances interfere with learning by interrupting the rhythm and thrust of curiosity.

Theories of learning range, of course, from the highly-structured behaviour-ism of B. F. Skinner (1968, 1971), through the *gestaltism* of Jerome Bruner (1977), to the extreme latitudinarianism of Carl Rogers (1969). It might seem that the position advocated here would identify most readily with Rogers's 'freedom to learn' as offering an image of the person freely deciding upon a line of enquiry and becoming personally enriched by the commitment undertaken. But this would be to oversimplify. If certain types of knowledge and skill are best acquired by the systematic application of a stimulus–response model, then it is wise to use that model for that purpose. Skinner's theories, which nourish much practice in programmed learning, can provide liberation for the person who enjoys the privacy of practising skills with a machine rather than in the perhaps unnecessary transaction with other people. Computers, after all, never get cross or have headaches. Unfortunately (for educational theory that is), higher education is only minimally concerned with the development of basic skills; it is much more concerned with the higher-level objectives (analysis, synthesis, etc.) of Bloom's *Taxonomy of Educational Objectives* (1956). These objectives are 'higher' only in a technical sense (involving greater levels of generality and abstraction), not in a 'moral' sense, although we often perversely equate abstraction with virtue.

It is not possible to teach without implicitly (if not explicitly) adopting some theory of learning. Many lecturers who profess themselves uninterested in learning theory in practice adopt (possibly by imitating what they experienced as students) a crude variant of the stimulus–response theory – perhaps assuming that lectures, for example, act as a stimulus to learning. There may be better ways to stimulate learning, but it is practically impossible to demonstrate this. Here is the great dilemma for anyone interested in a critical evaluation of teaching methods: 'target groups' for a particular type of instruction in higher education, contrasted with groups in secondary education, are too small for any generalizations to be made with safety. It is for precisely this reason that preferences (see below) are all that can be offered; and preferences imply some basis of moral judgement to be exercised largely in the absence of confirmation or disconfirmation of specific techniques from educational research.

Heresies

With the division of labour in society, and the consequent specialization of interests, there is a constant tendency for 'heresies' to spring up in the prescription of curricula, particularly perhaps in education for the professions. Each of the four listed here represents an attempt, in many ways laudable, to stress the importance of one or other aspect of curriculum or teaching method – but does so at the expense of the others. The letters after the heresies represent the quadrant of Figure 5.2 into which the 'heresy' has drifted.

Heresy 1: Determinism (A)

Belief in the exclusively social genesis of knowledge and overstatement of the (often undeniable) class interest in knowledge.

Curriculum planning, for example, drawing upon the fruitful (Marxist) notion that the superstructure of ideas is heavily dependent upon the activity of interest groups, becomes heretical whenever it is claimed that the curriculum is, could or should be entirely formed by social process. To deny the possibility or opportunity of individuals creating unique syntheses of ideas in their studies is fundamentally anti-humanist. Dr Johnson's tart comment: 'Sir, we *know* our will is free, and *there's* an end on't' may or may not be the last word on the question of free will versus determinism. But existentialist critics (Sartre,

Camus, Buber, Marcel and others) assert, as against determinists, that it is possible for individual insight to be valuable above the wisdom of committees.

The heresies which affect teaching methods are very similar to those which affect curriculum, which is not surprising, since form and content are inextricably intertwined. For example, overplanning of education, or overdependence on some theory of learning to the extent that the provisional and tentative nature of educational theory is lost to sight, may result from a purely social pressure to assert a style of instruction.

In this area, it is somewhat dispiriting to note that writers who have done signal service in alerting us to class interests in knowledge (e.g. Bourdieu and Passeron 1977; Bowles and Gintis 1976; Collins 1979; Sarup 1978; Sharp 1980; and the authors in Young (ed.) 1971) have not been very illuminating in suggesting how we may escape from the trap of 'What = Says Who?' (Cf. Berger and Luckmann 1967).

Heresy 2: Academicism (A/B)

Reification of knowledge, involved in the definition of disciplines as though the disciplines were somehow independent of the people who created them.

The phrase 'knowledge for its own sake' is sometimes a symptom of this heresy. Hirst (1974) comes pretty near to a restatement of Platonic idealism in his thesis about 'forms' and 'fields' of knowledge, although he denies commitment to any such position. Certainly with mathematics there is a givenness about the inner logic of the discipline which is compelling; but with every other type of knowledge, we fall back upon conventions of description and concentrations of interest, which, while in their more highly developed forms relatively inaccessible to those not versed in the disciplines, are ultimately traceable to individual or social concerns. In many ways, academicism is antithetical to determinism, but only as a competitor – urging the apparent immovability of subject matter.

A very common symptom of academicism is the assertion that if students are to be properly educated it is necessary to 'cover the ground' (whatever that may mean). The baleful consequence can be that syllabuses become cluttered with so many facts that students have neither the time nor the opportunity to reflect on the meaning the subject might have for them personally or for society more widely.

The heresy of academicism is found in teaching methods whenever there is over-emphasis of systems of thought, concepts or intellectual structures to the neglect of the contextual details which alone can give them meaning.

Academicism in teaching is informed by the valid notion that a major (if not *the* major) contribution of academic disciplines to our understanding of the world is the power of their organizing concepts. Disciplines bring order by limiting the field and method of observation. It is easy to slide into the belief that the concepts are in some way 'better' than the details they help us to comprehend, even that people who analyse, classify, and observe are in some way more noble than those who produce, initiate and do. While it is hard to conceive of education which does not involve abstracting ideas from detail, education which concentrates exclusively on this is to be avoided.

Heresy 3: Utilitarianism (C)

The adaptationist tendency to see learning always as a means to some social end, concerned with practice, never as a source of personal enlightenment, revelation or satisfaction to the individual.

The utilitarian heresy is in constant danger of appearing whenever manpower-planning goals come to dominate educational thinking. It appears in quadrant 'C' because it is often the result of well-meaning committee work which tidies out of existence the slow, muddled, baroque quality of learning which may involve 'playing with ideas' or the simple accumulation of information for delight. If the desire for social relevance in studies is kept in balance with other factors it can be a considerable source of wisdom; total absorption with quadrant 'C' is stultifying.

In teaching, utilitarianism appears as an over-emphasis on the practical 'needs of society' (or industry) or on the 'demands of scholarship' in specifying types of learning to be undertaken. By contrast, the techniques of research, scholarship and reflection (through which 'content' or 'curriculum' are organized) are the tools of trade of the academic occupation. As soon as these tools of the trade become advocated for their own sake, one is into the heresy of academicism. Symptoms of the heresy are found in mutterings about the need for 'rigour' – as though that were an end in itself and not the means towards some other end.

Heresy 4: Mechanism (C)

The vice of treating persons as part of some system or organization, neglecting other dimensions of their personality.

Mechanism is in quadrant 'C', being the characteristic vice of manpower planners and trainers of one sort and another. There is nothing intrinsically wrong with training: we need to submit to the prescriptions of those who have mastered techniques if we are to learn the techniques ourselves. Heresy creeps in when technique becomes the *primary* object of education.

Mechanism is, perhaps, most visible in vocational technical education; if students are treated *only* as intending engineers or physicists or whatever, with no encouragement or opportunity to develop any other interests in their studies, they are being treated as a means to some other end (supplying the manpower 'needs of industry' for example) rather than as persons. Mechanism, though less visible, is, however, present in the humanities too. If scholarship or research becomes reified, ('historical research requires . . .') people in higher education can slip into the heresy of forgetting what is the purpose of their work, letting work become the purpose of their lives. With an understandable instinct for survival, students can collude with mechanism by over-valuing education for supposedly supplying job skills (quadrant D).

The fact that mechanism often uses the language of fluid dynamics ('the flow of candidates', 'new blood'), rather than that of straight mechanics ('force', 'momentum', etc.) should not disguise its dehumanizing quality and fundamental illiberality.

Preferences

This section does not seek to prescribe a formula for curriculum design or teaching method; rather it mentions some preferences ('good practice' as it were) for *any* curriculum or teaching method in higher education. For clarity and economy of space the exampies relate to education for the professions. It cannot be emphasized too strongly that these remarks are about the curriculum and teaching methods in institutions specifically devoted to education. There are obviously institutional contexts in which learning (even teaching as such) takes place where it may be less necessary to seek such a balance, e.g. research institutes (perhaps concerned with pure theory) or factories (making items for daily use).

As already indicated (through the resistances implied by the identification of the heresies), preferences in teaching methods necessarily involve a search for the possibility of mutuality and debate, of two-way transaction in which lecturer and student learn from each other, rather than the *de haut en bas* posture of the teacher controlling the activity of the learner according to some plan of which the learner is left in ignorance.

Reflection and consultation

So easy is it to drift into one or other form of heresy, that the first desideratum for achieving academic freedom for teachers and taught is a reflective component in any course of study, an opportunity to be self-conscious and critically aware of *why* any particular component of the syllabus is there or what it is that one is seeking to achieve.

The 'theory' involved in higher education could, I have suggested above, be deemed its distinguishing feature. Teachers in higher education may not know more than the individual practitioner: the radio 'ham' may have more raw information than the electrical engineer, the antiquary more specific facts than the historian, and so on. I have argued elsewhere (Goodlad 1976) that teachers in higher education exhibit the defining characteristic of possessing 'authoritative uncertainty' when they know, on the basis of highly organized study, what it is worth trying to find out and why. They have, in short, a principle of selection. Their uncertainty is not the uncertainty of sheer ignorance, but rather the uncertainty of deep learning. For the student to come some way towards this experience of 'authoritative uncertainty' is a consummation devoutly to be wished: it is, perhaps, a defence against determinism and academicism.

One useful form of the experience of uncertainty can be generated by the application of ideas to new conditions – for example, through project work where the student has the opportunity to make a personal synthesis of ideas (Goodlad and Pippard 1982). What is important is for the student to experience the excitement and delight of trying to make sense of data by constructing or using concepts or hypotheses, even if these turn out to be 'wrong' when viewed from the vantage point of wider information. Undergraduate research opportunities, (MacVicar and McGavern 1984) have been provided, for example, at the Massachussetts Institute of Technology (MIT), to let students work alongside faculty and share some of the agony and ecstasy of work of this sort. One significant advantage of this type of work over traditional project work is that students can join an on-going programme rather than involve the faculty in the logistically complex task of finding chunks of do-able work which would fit into a given curriculum time-slot.

Another method of achieving the critical self-conscious 'cultural migration' from the orbit of one's main discipline is to view it from the perspective of another, from which the 'certainties' may look less certain. For this purpose, physics could be inspected from the perspective of philosophy, literature from anthropology, engineering from economics, philosophy from sociology, anthropology from history, etc. The 'disturbing' perspective will vary from discipline to discipline; some disciplines even provide their own, cf. the phenomenon of sociologies of sociology (Friedrichs 1972; Gouldner 1971). What is required in each case, however, is an attempt to stimulate in students an awareness of the strengths and weaknesses of specific intellectual positions.

If the tentative and provisional nature of intellectual perspectives is to be emphasized in the curriculum, it might seem strange to confront students with an elaborately structured curriculum. Just as the rationale for the *content* needs to be explained and subjected to critical appraisal, so should the *process* of instruction be exposed to criticism. Some form of deliberate and explicit consultation by teachers with students seems called for.

It may sound hopelessly Utopian to suggest such a process of consultation between teacher(s) and taught at the beginning of their acquaintanceship: how could the timetable, allocation of rooms, library purchases, etc. possibly be arranged if this were to take place? Is it not sufficient that students can make a 'market' choice between institutions and courses, whose operating style they can discover from a multitude of 'consumer' guides, before they apply? Perhaps: but consultation is a form of courtesy which needs to be extended whenever and wherever there is any room at all for manoeuvre. In most courses in higher education, there is very considerable room for manoeuvre.

Within conventional degree courses, it is becoming increasingly fashionable to provide 'study skills' courses to students, often in their first year, to help them to make the best use of their time and to learn how to get the most from the teaching methods offered. But just as it is somewhat shocking that the pastoral role of the faculty has collapsed to such an extent that professional counselling services are nowadays found to be necessary in most colleges, so it should be seen as a symptom of illiberality that 'study skills' courses are deemed desirable. Even if logistic considerations demand that degree courses are not dismantled and reassembled within the first weeks of an academic year, it is at least desirable that some dialogue should take place between teachers and students about the purpose and plan of a course, and about how the students may best use what is offered (often, in practice, relating the theory they are being offered to the practice with which they identify). If properly used, study skills sessions could become a useful point of discussion between teachers and students about the rationale for the teaching methods of the course.

Problem-based study

One of the potentially most fruitful ways of maintaining the balance between theory and practice, society and the individual, is that of problem-based study. Very often, of course, project work is problem-based; but not all problem-based study is project work. For example, the Macmaster Medical School (Barrows and Tamblyn 1980; Neufeld and Chong 1984) arranges for students to learn medicine by confronting a graded series of problems of patient-care. The procedure was adopted originally both because it was clear that students quickly forgot what they heard in parallel, theory-based lecture courses; and students who were going to have to practise as professionals, often isolated from the support of a medical school, needed to learn how to learn, so that they could cope with new situations and the massive yearly increase in medical knowledge mediated to them through floods of journal articles and the promotional literature of drug companies. Accordingly, students are not given lectures; rather they are presented (through live interviews, simulations, and other methods) with the sort of multidimensional problems encountered in practice – for example, chest pains which may have complex social, psychological and physiological causes. Students can draw upon whatever resources of medical theory or practical investigation that they think may help; but always they have to remain aware of the costs of what they undertake (the financial accountability involved in ordering more tests than are necessary, and the moral responsibility of ordering fewer). By this method, which seems to be both efficient in producing graduates with few drop-outs and popular as a recruiting device for students, some of the more serious curricular heresies may be avoided. Interestingly, the Macmaster Medical School also respects the interests and needs of the individual student by providing option courses in which students, freed from the encounter with graded problems, can follow an interest wherever it may lead. Boud (1985) offers a useful survey of how problem-based learning is developing in other professions.

The academic freedom of students to learn and of faculty to teach implies liberality in administration; curriculum, by contrast, implies control. There need be no conflict: it is only *rigidity*, often lurking behind control, that is the source of much heresy. Rigidity is fundamentally antipathetic to the humanistic perspective here advanced because it involves the denial of persons, the rejection of conviviality and mutuality through a mistaken pride in the viewpoint of the person exercising control. The very process of institutionalization involved in organizing individual learning by the device of curriculum carries the danger of each type of heresy discussed above.

If measurement could be carried out of learning acquired other than under the immediate direction, control and supervision of college teachers, considerable loosening of heresy-heavy rigidities could be contemplated. Happily, much work is currently going on in this area, some of it pioneered in the United States by the Council for the Advancement of Experiential Learning (CAEL), which has evolved techniques for accrediting learning acquired outside formal educational settings, through life and/or work experience, through study service or service learning, etc. (see, for example, Willingham 1977; Doyle and Chickering 1982). The applications of this concept, as Evans (1981, 1983) has shown, are many and various; the retrospective analysis of knowledge and skills acquired in non-formal learning settings could permit, *inter alia*, freedom of movement between occupations, late entry into higher education (and/or into new jobs) without the individual having to go back to square one, credit or transfer between institutions.

Experiential learning, if retrospectively analysed and accredited, is obviously to be preferred for the freedom of movement it offers. The principle of systematic analysis of what has been learned rather than the prescription of what has to be learned is also the animating force behind schools of Independent Study, such as that at the North East London Polytechnic (Percy and Ramsden 1980).

Engagement reflection modes of study

To avoid the dangers of the heresies sketched above, a teaching method is desirable which combines theory with practice, and which recognizes students' obligations both to themselves, in terms of nourishing the imagination and sense of individuality, and to 'society' in the sense of offering opportunity to relate studies directly or indirectly to the interests and needs of the community which is paying for those studies.

Problem-based study, including project work, can in principle fruitfully link theory and practice; it can also nourish individual initiative. Projects are, of course, undertaken for clients (for example, industrial projects by engineering students); where this is done, the intention is often to expose students to the interests, needs or preoccupations of some constituency for which the students' theoretical studies are arranged. The 'danger', of course, is that problems are often (if not usually) selected for projects which are in principle soluble. Many problems, however, are not soluble – at least not in a project lasting three months in the final year of an undergraduate's studies. A form of study may be required which allows students to engage with difficult situations and then to reflect upon them. In this way, one might hope to avoid the heresy of academicism. One example of 'good practice', which is attractive from the perspective advocated in this paper, is that of Study Service.

Study Service is the term applied by UNESCO to work in which students combine study leading to the award of an academic qualification with some form of direct practical service to the community. Students in Study Service schemes do not compete with paid professionals; rather, *they do work which could not otherwise have been done*. There are abundant examples of ways in which students have rendered direct, practical service as part of their study (Goodlad 1982). Students have designed and made devices for the handicapped, under-taken 'consultancy' work, carried out surveys, assisted teachers in schools by 'tutoring', worked in preventive medicine projects, assisted in rural develop-ment, carried out 'advocacy' work in planning enquiries, and so forth. The key feature of Study Service is that students are given some direct, personal responsibility towards someone else – so that, in fact, their 'study' is not simply for personal satisfaction or advancement but is *simultaneously* useful to someone else. Not only does the interweaving of engagement (through the placement) and reflection (through study) provide an opportunity for the integration of theory and practice, but the development of individual persons is also under-taken in a context which offers fruitful contact with one or other of the many agencies through which 'Society' (otherwise a watery abstraction of textbooks) operates.

Some principles of good practice

In the perspective developed in this paper, academic freedom is seen not as the total absence of constraints but rather as a holding together of the notions of theory and practice, society and the individual in as many facets as possible of education for the professions. The principle of trust requires that in a system which is inevitably layered, those in the 'higher' layers (i.e. having the greater power of control) should place the greatest possible trust in those in the layers below them. If the *aims and objects* of specific actions are established clearly and freely and willingly accepted, there will be administrative efficiency through the shortening of the lines of communication.

Although space does not permit detailed elaboration of these notions, it should be clear that the position concerning academic freedom advocated in this paper points to certain preferences in areas not so far touched, examples of which are given below.

Public Sector Higher Education: annual monitoring survey

The present basis of this major 'indicator of performance' is class contact. Staff–student ratios are calculated with a formula which puts a premium on institutions not only increasing class sizes, but also demonstrating the highest possible number of hours for students attending classes and lecturers teaching them. This system of monitoring is *BAD* because it biases the system *away* from greater independence in study. Lecturers might be better employed in further-ing their knowledge by research, consultancy or private study and in planning work for students to do (updating reading lists, problems sheets, laboratory experiments) than in instructing students directly. Similarly, students might be better employed working on their own, using well-planned materials, than in simply being present in the same rooms as the lecturers because the accounting system requires it. Not only does the monitoring system currently bias the mode of instruction towards potential inefficiency and ineffectiveness; it also need-lessly inhibits institutions' freedom in teaching (cell G of Figure 5.1). Trust gives place to a crudely mechanical form of accountability.

The Polytechnics and Colleges Funding Council (PCFC) and Universities Funding Council (UFC)

These councils, proposed in the Education Reform Bill and currently in process of being set up, are to operate through a system of 'contracts' with educating institutions. At the time of writing, it is not at all clear how this system will operate. The rhetoric is in terms of freeing institutions, particularly those in the public sector of higher education, from bureaucratic entanglements; but what is currently proposed looks more likely to bring about increased centralization of planning through the power of the PCFC or UFC to give or withhold 'con-tracts'. Apart from the danger that administrative intelligence often becomes cruder the further it gets from the chalk face, increased centralization of control is *BAD* because it removes responsibility from institutions, thereby showing lack of trust in them by agencies higher up the system. If the object being sought is greater accountability of institutions for their use of public funds, that can as well be served by requiring them to publish their accounts. If 'value for money' is being sought, that object may better be achieved by a complex network of funding arrangements with some sort of 'court' in which those with grievances, including the Secretary of State, can get a proper hearing with adjustment of procedures as appropriate. This way, one puts trust in *everyone* to do their best. Both the University Grants Committee (UGC) and the National Advisory Body for Public Sector Higher Education (NAB) operated in this way. The Board of the NAB was more like a 'court' than anything in the UGC, although the UGC's complex network of subject committees served much the same purpose.

Formula funding at departmental level

This is now widely adopted in universities. It can be *BAD* if it generates competitive disarray between departments in the pursuit of FTEs (full-time equivalent students). Interdisciplinary study, project work crossing departmental boundaries, service teaching designed to introduce an element of reflection into single-subject disciplines – these activities, usually designed to ensure the liberal education of students in the ways advocated in this paper, are all under threat from administrative rigidities which systematically subvert any process of collegial responsibility. Formulae can provide admirable *maps* for planning purposes; computerized information systems based on them can also offer the possibility of 'what if' speculation about the adventurous use of resources. But for the management of an institution to adopt formula funding *without* the possibility of exercising discretion and flexibility within the overall funding regime is again to substitute a crudely mechanical system for one based upon trust that people, even collectively under financial pressure, can reach sound judgements.

Two-year first degrees

These have been under discussion for nearly twenty years; they were, for example, advocated strongly in the Society for Research into Higher Education study *Excellence in Diversity* (1983). In the perspective of this paper, they would be *GOOD* because they would offer three students the chance of two years' study rather than two students three years' study. Experience with the DipHE, for example, in the School for Independent Study at the North East London Polytechnic, suggests that two-year degrees could be made to work without dilution of academic standards if greater use were to be made of part-time, independent study to 'top up' two-year (pass) degrees into honours degrees.

Administrative arrangements such as these, upon which most contemporary debate focuses, are only means to the end or aim of nourishing persons. If we are clear in our minds about what *that* involves we will know when, how and where to defend academic freedom.

Note

1 The argument here draws on discussions I have enjoyed with the Trustees of the Higher Education Foundation. They must not, however, be held responsible for any infelicities or naivetes in it. In addition, I am grateful to the Trustees of the Higher Education Foundation for financial help towards the cost of study in 1983, 1984 and 1985, and to the Center for Studies at the University of California, Berkeley, for facilities and intellectual stimulus during my stay there as Visiting Associate in 1983 that helped me to make best use of the munificence of the Higher Education Foundation.

6

Free Speech and the Universities

Bhikhu Parekh

During the past few years scores of visiting speakers to our universities have been abused, shouted down or otherwise ill-treated and prevented from speaking on the grounds that they canvassed fascist, racist and other types of morally offensive doctrines. The protests were not confined to the anarchists and the so-called extreme left. Even the much-admired 'moderate' champions of freedom of speech thought that the university ought not to offer a 'platform' to such speakers.[1]

The 'no-platform' policy has been condemned by the champions of what I might call 'open-door policy' on the grounds that it betrays intolerance, bigotry and dogmatism and contradicts the nature of the university as a rational institution committed to untrammelled inquiry. In partial response to their pressure the government has recently passed a law imposing on the university authorities the obligation to take all reasonable measures to ensure that invited speakers are in no way ill-treated or prevented from speaking. The law, however, leaves the universities free to work out their own mechanisms for deciding whom to invite. As in all such controversies, neither side has the monopoly of truth. In this paper I intend to outline and assess the validity of the arguments on which the cases for the two policies rest.

Open door policy

The advocates of 'open-door' policy defend it on a number of grounds of which the following two are the most important. The first argument is general in nature and invokes the principle of free speech.

Based on the familiar views of Milton, Locke and especially J. S. Mill, they defend free speech on such grounds as that it is self-justifying, a matter of natural right, the necessary basis of rationality, an indispensable precondition of the search for truth, a necessary safety value and a vital means of human progress. Since it is highly desirable it is only to be curtailed when likely to lead to socially harmful action.[2] It is the job of the law to specify which utterances under what conditions are likely to have such consequences, and therefore like all other freedoms, freedom of speech is necessarily limited by the law. Since freedom of speech within the law is desirable in society as a whole, it is also by definition desirable in the university. Any section of the university must therefore enjoy the freedom to invite whoever they like, and the university has a duty to ensure him or her a peaceful hearing.

The second argument is advanced in the specific context of the university. Of all social institutions the university is unique in being concerned with the pursuit and propagation of knowledge. It critically examines ideas and beliefs, assesses evidence and arguments both for and against them and aims to arrive at a 'true' or rationally defensible view on the subject in question. No body of ideas or beliefs falls or should fall outside its purview. To shut them out is to betray dogmatism and arbitrarily to restrict the spirit of critical inquiry. Furthermore the university consists of reasonably mature people already trained or currently being trained in the craft of critically sifting ideas, and one can depend on them not to be swayed by flimsy or untenable doctrines. Compared to other institutions the university should therefore practise *greater* freedom of speech and open its doors to anybody who has anything to say.

Both arguments make valid points but draw invalid conclusions. Take the first argument. Even if we granted that the case for freedom of speech in general rests on logically impeccable grounds and that it is highly desirable, it is not clear how it entails an open door policy.[3] As the advocates of the policy rightly argue, the university is an academic institution concerned to discover and transmit knowledge. As an academic institution only academic discourse has a place in it, and it has a duty to ensure that no unjustified restrictions are imposed upon such discourse. This means, conversely, that non-academic discourse has no place in the university and the latter remains free to forbid or restrict it. While the university should encourage the free flow of academic discourse and the visits of academic and academically relevant speakers, it may legitimately and consistently forbid or restrict purely political speakers speaking on purely political issues in a highly partisan manner. Such speakers do not speak an academic language, have no interest in or competence to handle academic discourse, and have nothing to contribute to academic inquiry, and hence they do not belong to the university. It may invite them if it so pleases, but it has no obligation to do so and is not being untrue to itself if it does not.

The second argument is open to a similar objection. Since the university institutionalizes reason and is committed to untrammelled rational inquiry, two conclusions follow. First, reason alone is entitled to be heard in the university; that is, only those who are willing to argue, persuade and be persuaded are entitled to its hospitality. Second, unreason is welcome only if it is willing to submit itself to the sustained and searching scrutiny of reason. The bulk of racist and fascist speakers whose presence on the campus is under dispute do not satisfy either condition. Their discourse is suffused with unsubstantiated assertions, unexamined prejudices, wild exaggerations and crude abuses, and could hardly be called rational. Even then they could and should be invited by the university if they were able and prepared to engage in a critical dialogue with others in a seminar-type situation. Martin Webster and Harvey Proctor are welcome to the university to read a paper before a student or staff seminar. The fact of the matter is that these men studiously avoid such typically academic situations, being concerned only to harangue large crowds and mobilize the faithful. It is precisely because the university is devoted to rational inquiry that it may consistently deny its hospitality to those not in the least interested in such an inquiry.

The open door policy then is not tenable; at any rate its advocates have advanced no arguments to convince us that it is. Their case rests on a series of illicit extrapolations. The fact that the university should show utmost tolerance towards *academic* speech does not mean that it should tolerate *all* forms of speech including the unacademic. The fact that it is committed to rational discussion does not mean that it may not close its doors to those uninterested in or opposed to it. And the fact that it impartially examines all kinds of *ideas*, including fascism and racism, does not mean that it may not close its doors to their *spokesmen*. The university, indeed, should store their literature and teach their ideas, yet it may with perfect consistency deny its hospitality to their crude peddlers and cruder practitioners.

'No platform' policy

Let us now turn to the 'no platform' policy. Its advocates defend it on several grounds of which the following are most common. First, the university is an academic institution devoted to critical and impartial investigation of ideas. Political speakers devoid of academic interest or competence have no place in it and ought not to be invited. Since they have nothing to contribute to academic life, those inviting them are almost by definition only motivated by a political desire to help them propagate their ideas and to lend them the university's moral authority. Protests against such speakers are intended to affirm the academic character of the university and are directed as much against them as against their misguided hosts.

Second, the university is not a mere collection of people but a community whose smooth functioning requires a climate of mutual respect, trust and good will. Relations between its members are necessarily delicate and require careful cultivation. A racist or an antisemitic speaker who subjects blacks and Jews to ridicule, contempt or hated, denouncing the former as savages, stupid and carriers of AIDS and the latter as devious, rapacious, contemptible and thoroughly deserving of Hitler's wrath, triggers off deep prejudices and fears, introduces a disturbing note of tension in their relations and undermines the inherently precarious climate of civility that the university has taken years to develop.

Third, as a body of men and women trained to take a long-term view of their society and civilization, the university has a duty to ensure that it does not become an unwitting accomplice to the creation of forces likely to subvert their very foundation. We know that Hitler came to power in Germany because, among other things, the universities allowed themselves to be used by him and his followers. In the name of academic neutrality the universities threw open their doors to them, boosted their morale and self-confidence and enabled them to brainwash and even recruit staff and students. It is about time we learned the tragic lessons of the 'open door' policy.

Finally, one may not oneself be in favour of a 'no platform' policy. However, if one has reason to believe that some groups of students feel deeply offended and threatened by certain types of speaker, one has as a member of the privileged majority a duty to reassure and show one's solidarity with them by denying the objectionable speakers a platform or protesting against their presence. The protest cannot be left to the minority groups alone for they are too weak to stand up for themselves and cannot be expected to invite embarrassing ridicule and abuse.

Let us briefly examine each argument in turn. The first argument makes a valid point, which I raised earlier against the 'open door' policy. The university *is* an academic place devoted to the discussion of academic issues in a calm atmosphere. There is an important distinction between talking politics and talking about politics, speaking a racist language and speaking about racism, and the university is basically concerned with the latter. It has, therefore, no obligation to invite political speakers and it is not being untrue to its basic objectives if it does not invite them. However, since it is an academic institution concerned to discuss and analyse ideas current in the society at large, there is no obvious reason why it may not invite political speakers, engage them in a dialogue and subject their ideas to a critical interrogation. Ugly ideas do not disappear by shutting one's eyes to them, and there is no better place than the university to expose their moral pathology.

The university *may* therefore invite their advocates if the two conditions listed earlier are satisfied: that is, if they are willing and able to defend their views by means of rational argument and if there is an opportunity to question and enter into a dialogue with them. Powell and Eysenck, who have both been wholly undeserved victims of the 'no-platform' policy, eminently satisfy the first condition, whereas Webster and Proctor do not. And even the former may be invited only if they are prepared to answer questions and rationally defend their views. Although not always easy to apply in practice, it is essential to draw a distinction between advocacy and incitement. Advocacy is a quasi-theoretical exercise and involves a reasoned defence of a body of ideas. Incitement is a wholly practical activity uninterested in rational argument and designed only to encourage action. Subject to the conditions discussed later, the university may and indeed should give unlimited scope to advocacy, but none at all to incitement.

The second argument raises important questions whose gravity is not fully appreciated by the liberal critics of 'no platform' policy. The university *is* a community and requires a climate of mutual trust and civility. It is also a place where students drawn from different social backgrounds, nationalities and races have a unique opportunity to interact, get to know one another and build up friendships across racial, ethnic and class barriers. Any external intervention likely to damage this ought to be viewed with disfavour. Academic activity, further, requires propitious conditions, and obviously students feeling intensely nervous, unsettled and edgy by a periodic barrage of racist, fascist and other forms of propaganda are hardly in a position to concentrate on their work. Advocates of the 'no-platform' policy are right to argue that black and Jewish students do feel not only offended but also emotionally threatened and even physically insecure when a member of the National Front or other similar organization visits their university, especially as they cannot be sure what reactions he will trigger off among the rest of the student body. It is worth noting that the 'no platform' policy became popular in the 1970s in the aftermath of some vicious attacks on black and Jewish students.

Although there is a genuine danger of outside speakers vitiating the tranquil life of the university, it cannot be met by a blanket ban on racist and fascist speakers. As we saw earlier, reasoned advocacy is very different from incitement. Unlike Proctor, Webster and others who are only interested in, and sometimes do succeed in, stirring up trouble, Powell, Eysenck and others present nuanced and well-considered views which, however mistaken, do not have this result. Much, of course, depends on the prevailing climate in the university. In some circumstances, such as when racial incidents have occurred there and feelings are running high, even the visit of Powell and Eysenck may be banned. That they may *then* be denied a platform does not justify a *blanket* ban on their visits.

The third argument advanced by the advocates of the 'no platform' policy is the least persuasive. It rests on a false reading of the German experience. There is no evidence that the Nazis made much use of universities or that they would not have come to power had the universities denied a platform to some of their leaders. It also rests on a mistaken reading of contemporary Britain for, again, there is no evidence that the racist groups are drawing their recruits from the universities or that their current popularity owes anything to their visits to them.

The last argument makes a valid point but exaggerates its importance. Victims of racist abuse do need support and protection, and the moral concern underlying the 'no platform' policy is well-grounded. However such a concern has little meaning if it remains confined to the university. The blacks and Jews are far more worried about the racism and antisemitism prevalent in society at large than in the visits of their spokesmen to the university. They sometimes feel that some of the champions of the 'no platform' policy do not seem to be much concerned about the former, and that their attempts to shout down speakers represent a form of cutting moral corners and contain a measure of self-deception.

The question, ultimately, is whether the 'no platform' policy is achieving the desired results. The answer is largely in the negative. The detested speakers continue to sell their offensive wares; the law remains unchanged; the universities get a bad name; and the blacks in whose name the rumpus is created are made to look intolerant. Indeed, the policy seems to have produced the opposite results to those intended, and has given rise to a new breed of professional martyr.

The game is simple and its rules are transparent. Take a job in a sensitive area. After a while make a few silly remarks or sensible remarks in a wrong context. When your victims are compelled to protest, start complaining about being harassed and persecuted, making sure that your murmur catches the highly sensitive ears of the organized lobby only too ready to lend its support to your cause. You, whom no one had noticed before, are suddenly a hero, a forlorn champion of civilized values and eventually a martyr. You agree to leave your job only after you are offered a princely sum. You collect the money and the contrived invitations of wholly unrepresentative groups of sympathetic students, do rounds of universities where your heroism and martyrdom are resented by the vociferous champions of the 'no platform' policy. Their attempts to shout you down enhance your heroic qualities, deepen your hollow halo of martyrdom and earn you yet more lucrative contracts for articles and interviews in the news-manipulating media. If you have any integrity you will, of course, feel deeply disturbed that you are being used and turned into an object of consumption and will be discarded once the last drop of your energy is squeezed out of you. Most, however, are not in the least bothered and enjoy their brief moments of glory and hefty earnings. It is not at all clear to me how encouraging such crass vulgarity and promoting a grotesque black-baiting industry helps the anti-racist cause or its intended beneficiaries.

Advocates of the 'open door' policy have sometimes advanced two criticisms of the 'no platform' policy. First, it is morally selective in that it condemns racism and fascism but not the equally offensive left-wing doctrines. Second, such terms as racism and fascism are not easy to define and become excuses for banning everybody of whose views or policies one disapproves. Neither criticism is persuasive. Victims of racism and antisemitism carry their identity on their face and are easy to identify and attack. This cannot be said of capitalists, reactionaries and other targets of left-wing attacks. Furthermore, unlike the capitalists and others whose identity is defined by their beliefs and practices, and hence is alterable, the blacks and Jews are such by virtue of their natural properties and can do nothing to alter their identity. Racism, fascism and antisemitism are therefore qualitatively different from left-wing ideologies. This is not to say that the latter may not lead to an equally great or even greater evil, only that there is a fundamental logical difference between the two, and that a policy that bans one but not the other is not guilty of inconsistency.

As for the second criticism, it misses the point and makes the all too common mistake of confusing theoretical with practical difficulty. The question is not one of *defining* racism, fascism or antisemitism but of *specifying* their most inhuman and offensive forms, and that can be done, as it has been done, with relative ease. Furthermore, the fact that we cannot offer incontestable and universally compelling definitions of these terms does not mean that we cannot identify their paradigmatic forms. After all, the fact that we cannot offer such definitions of freedom and right has never prevented the law from granting and us from enjoying them. In philosophy we are concerned to determine the boundaries as well as the central and paradigmatic usages of concepts. In practical life only the easily identifiable centres of activities concern us. The conceptual difficulties facing a philosopher rarely confront us in practical life, and hence to extrapolate *his* problem to the latter is to be guilty of a serious muddle and to commit what I might call the fallacy of theoreticism. As St Augustine said: 'I may not be able to tell you *what time is*, but I can easily tell you *what time it is*.'

A simple principle

In the light of this discussion we arrive at a simple principle. The university is an academic institution in the sense of being concerned with a rational and impartial pursuit of knowledge. In deciding whether or not to invite speakers, the only question it must ask is whether they are capable of participating in and contributing to academic discourse on the relevant subject. If the answer is in the affirmative, it has a duty to invite them. If it is in the negative, it has no such duty, although it does not have a duty not to invite them either. Its decision then is entirely prudential and based on a sensitive calculus of advantages.

The 'open door' policy then is right in relation to those capable of enriching the university's academic life. The 'no platform' policy is right in relation to those who have no academic competence and interest, are only concerned to incite ill-feeling against identifiable groups, and are known to be connected with agitationally orientated organizations whether of the left or of the right. In denying its hospitality to such men and women, the university does not in the slightest degree compromise its commitment to academic freedom or violate the principle of free speech. At the same time, in denying it to those capable of participating in and enriching academic discourse, however mistaken and offensive their views might be, the university betrays its soul and undermines the basic conditions of its existence. The distinction is sometimes difficult to draw and mistakes are inevitable. A university must ultimately be judged not by its occasional and unavoidable lapses but by the sincerity of its commitment to the principle underlying the distinction.

Notes

1 The term platform is highly suggestive and implies that the speakers invited are deemed to be politically motivated and only concerned to propagate specific political doctrines.
2 The view that speech should be curtailed only when likely to lead to undesirable action is open to several objections. First, it does not judge speech in its own terms but exclusively from the standpoint of action. As a result it ignores the fact that certain types of utterance are inherently unacceptable; for example, those that demean and ridicule other men or groups, diminish and degrade them in their own and others' eyes, and/or undermine their self-respect and self-esteem. Second, it wrongly assumes that the harm caused by action is more serious than that caused by speech. Third, it rests on a dubious theory of causality, and requires that speech should be curtailed only when it can be shown *directly* to lead to an *identifiable* action. Such direct or immediate causality is never to be found in any area of life. Actions do not occur in a

vacuum. They presuppose a specific intellectual climate or context of ideas in which they are conceived, gestated, planned and legitimized. The intellectual climate is created and sustained by hosts of utterances, each of them making an intangible and not easily determinable but nevertheless definite contribution to it. That a specific action cannot be traced to a specific utterance does not means that it cannot be traced to a specific *class* of utterances *over a period of time*. In any discussion of human affairs we therefore need a rich and complex conception of causality based on structural mediations, temporality and classes of actions. The simple-minded and episodic view which requires direct and unmediated relations between two distinct events is false, ideologically biased and a source of much confusion.

3 I have argued elsewhere that speech is an abstraction and that different forms of speech raise distinct problems and require different types of justification. Freedom of the press, an organized and politically powerful mode of communication reaching out to millions with the authority inherent in a printed word, raises very different problems to the freedom of individuals to say what they like in their day-to-day relations (see Twitchin 1988, p. 85).

7

Human Rights and Academic Freedom

Margherita Rendel

By academic freedom I understand the right to search for the truth and to publish and teach what one holds to be true. This right also implies a duty: one must not conceal any part of what one has recognized to be true. It is evident that any restriction of academic freedom serves to restrain the dissemination of knowledge, thereby impeding rational judgement and action.

(Albert Einstein, quoted in Boudin 1983)

Nearly everyone is in favour of academic freedom in principle, though some would dissent from some of the provisions in Einstein's definition. Not all would agree, for example, that individual academics had a right to publish and teach what they held to be true when that conflicted with the views of, say, the Church or the Party or with the existing social and economic structure.

In this paper, I shall examine the contribution that human rights provisions can make to academic freedom, discuss the relationship between individual academic freedom and institutional autonomy, and consider the role of institutions of higher education in legitimating knowledge and licensing persons, a role which can contribute to maintaining the existing hegemony or offer scope for exploring alternative interpretations of society. I shall look briefly at the ideological, managerial and financial attacks on academic freedom and conclude by arguing that tenure is as necessary for institutional autonomy as for individual academic freedom, and that a Charter of Rights and Obligations for Academic Freedom is needed. I begin with the 'ingredients' of academic freedom.

The ingredients of academic freedom

Academic freedom for an institution usually includes autonomy or self-government according to the terms of its constitution, with power to determine academic policies, the balance between teaching and research, staffing ratios, the appointment, promotion and discipline of staff at all levels, the admission and discipline of students, curricula, standards, examinations and the conferring of degrees and diplomas; and with control over the material resources needed to undertake these activities.[1]

Some of these functions, especially the personnel functions, are common to most employers. Like any other body or organization, academia may fail to use these powers wisely or may abuse them, for example by appointing or promoting the unworthy, unjustly penalizing or disadvantaging able staff, discriminating unfairly among classes of students or staff, refusing to teach or research new subjects, neglecting those that are necessary, continuing subjects that should be abandoned or reduced, or otherwise mismanaging their affairs. The judgements about such decisions are nearly always value judgements and therefore provide scope for conflict in assessment.

Academic freedom for the individual has normally been associated with higher education and those in higher education, but others might claim it, for example teachers in other levels of education and research workers. So too might students: *Lernfreiheit* as well as *Lehrfreiheit*. Other groups in society may have a specific interest in academic freedom, for example minority, ethnic or handicapped groups who have been or are denigrated and who need the record to be corrected and the consequences of that correction to be fully drawn out. Similarly, women have an interest in the free development of women's studies.

Academic freedom for the academics is generally assumed to include the right to participate in the government of the institution and its policy-making, freedom in what and how to teach, choice of research topics, and freedom to travel and to communicate with colleagues. It also includes some choice of whom to teach, which must mean both a right, reasonably exercised, to reject potential students and a duty not to exclude unfairly or unreasonably suitable students from access to teachers or the institution.

These freedoms are assumed to be safeguarded by the grant of tenure to teachers (and occasionally to researchers) who have successfully completed a period of probation. Tenure has been in effect a status which the teacher could take to a new post and retain on promotion until retirement. Academics are not the only workers to enjoy tenure or something akin to it.[2] The present government's Education Reform Bill would deny tenure to those appointed after 20 November 1987 and would reduce 'good cause' to reasons related to capability, qualifications and conduct as defined and interpreted in the law relating to unfair dismissal. Under that law swearing or being difficult to work with have been held to be good grounds for dismissal. At present, tenured staff can be dismissed for gross misconduct or gross incompetence and a few are each year. Like institutions, academics may fail to carry out their duties, for example by laziness, neglecting their students or treating them unfairly, deliberately teaching unjustly biased material, or failing to do research. What is perceived as 'unjustly biased' depends on the location of the person making the judgement. It is therefore wiser to protect the expression of a wide plurality of views than to seek impartiality. Neither institutional autonomy nor tenure prevent action from being taken on inadequate performance.

Human rights instruments

I turn now to provisions in human rights documents that can be relevant to academic freedom. These documents do not deal specifically with academic freedom, but they do deal with non-discrimination, freedom of thought, freedom of expression, freedom to travel, the right to education and the right to work, all of which are relevant to academic freedom (see Brownlie 1971, 1981; Sieghart 1983).

Virtually all human rights instruments contain a provision banning discrimination. The most common formulation is that of the Universal Declaration of Human Rights 1948 (UDHR), Article 2: that each person should enjoy the rights provided for in the instrument 'without distinction of any kind such as race, colour, sex, language, religion, political or other opinion, national or social origin, property, birth or other status'. This list does not specifically mention age, disability, marital status or sexual orientation, although all of these could be covered by the final catch-all phrase.

The right to freedom of thought, conscience and religion is safeguarded in six instruments. Of these, four, the UDHR Article 18, the International Covenant on Civil and Political Rights 1966 (ICPR) Article 18, the European Convention on Human Rights and Fundamental Freedoms 1950 (EHR) Article 9 and its First Protocol 1952 (P1) Article 2, and the American Convention on Human Rights 1969 (AMR) Article 12, include 'beliefs' along with religion. It is clear from the context and from case-law, for example that of the European Court of Human Rights (EUCT), that philosophical beliefs come within the ambit of these provisions (Humphrey, 1984: 178). These four instruments also provide a right to teach or disseminate as well as to practise one's religion or beliefs, subject to respect for the human dignity of others. This caveat is most clearly spelt out in the EHR, Article 17.

For our purposes, the provisions concerning freedom of expression and opinion are more important. This right is dealt with in six documents. The UDHR Article 19, the American Declaration of Rights and Duties of Man 1948 (ADRD) Article IV, ICPR Article 19, EHR Article 10, AMR Article 13 and the African Charter on Human and People's Rights 1981 (AFR) Article 9 protect the right to hold, receive and impart information, and four of these UDHR, ADRD, ICPR and AMR – protect the further right to seek information or to investigate. There are safeguards for the rights and reputation of others, for national security, public order, public health and morals in the AMR, to which the EHR adds protection of information received in confidence and maintaining the authority and impartiality of the judiciary. Research would be covered by the right to seek information and to investigate. Students and colleagues would have a right to receive information. Teachers and researchers would have a right to impart information.

Aspects of the right to education are dealt with in a large number of documents. In general, these instruments are concerned with access to education, especially primary, elementary or basic education. Relatively little is said in them about higher education. The UDHR, the International Covenant on Economic, Social and Cultural Rights 1966 (ICES) Article 13 and the UNESCO Convention against Discrimination in Education 1960 Article 4 provide that higher education shall be equally accessible to all on merit, and ICES adds to this the progressive introduction of free higher education. Both the Declaration on Elimination of Discrimination against Women 1967 Article 9 and the Convention on the Elimination of All Forms of Discrimination against Women 1979 (CEDW) Article 13 safeguard women's access to education at all levels, to scholarships and study grants, examinations, teaching staff, qualifications and so on. The CEDW also requires the elimination of stereotyped concepts of the roles of men and women and the revision of textbooks, programmes and teaching methods accordingly. This last provision can be seen as a development of equivalent concepts in the International Convention on the Elimination of All Forms of Racial Discrimination 1966 Articles 4 and 7, which require States to take measures to combat prejudices leading to racial discrimination.

Regional instruments are also relevant: the Declaration of Punto del Este 1961 and the Charter of the Organization of American States (OAS), as amended by the Protocol of Buenos Aires 1967, urge States vastly to expand higher education, and both the OAS Charter as amended and the Helsinki Final Act 1975 are concerned with intellectual exchange and scientific (research and scholarly) activity. The Helsinki Final Act, which is not legally binding, provides for increased co-operation, exchanges, travel, access to information and so on for institutions and individuals concerned with scientific and academic work. The First Protocol 1952 of the EHR (P1) Article 2 provides a general right to education and requires States to respect the right of parents to ensure that state education and teaching are in conformity with the parents' own religious and philosophical convictions.

The right to work is protected in five documents: UDHR Article 23, ADRD Articles XIV and XXXVII, ICES Article 6, the European Social Charter 1961 (ESC) Part I(1) and Part II, Article I(1), and AFR Articles 15 and 29. Both the ADRD and the AFR lay a duty on individuals to work, and all except the AFR specify that individuals have a right to earn their living in an occupation freely entered upon. Both the ICES and the ESC lay upon States the obligation to pursue policies of full employment. The ESC provisions, like those in many Conventions of the International Labour Organization, are primarily concerned with non-discrimination, trade union rights, health and safety at work and such like. Nonetheless, the Charter could be interpreted as laying on governments an obligation to seek to maintain full employment for academics or ex-academics in occupations freely entered upon.

The right to travel is safeguarded by Article 2 of the Fourth Protocol 1963 (P4) of the EHR. This includes both the right to travel freely (have liberty of movement) within a State and the right to be free to leave any country, including one's own. As might be expected, these provisions are subject to qualifications such as being lawfully in the country and not being wanted by the police for crime or as a threat to national security. The United Kingdom has not yet ratified this Protocol.

At first view, human rights instruments appear to cover many of the ingredients of academic freedom, although academic freedom has to be read into other rights. It can be seen as a composite right rather than as a specific right. This is not surprising since in Britain the struggle for freedom of expression dates from the sixteenth century at least, and that for equal access for women and minorities to higher education still continues. The human rights instruments address ideological restraints on academic freedom and some practical restraints such as the right to travel, but, inevitably perhaps, they do little to ensure that the material needs of academics and of academic institutions are met. Similarly, while the instruments condemn discrimination, and disqualification, with few exceptions they do little to promote positive action to assist members of disadvantaged groups to enjoy academic freedom at any level.

How useful a right is depends on its enforceability. Declarations, which are not enforceable, have a certain value for legitimating pressure for more effective action. Covenants and Conventions are enforceable only against States which have ratified or otherwise signalled their adherence to them. There are two broad types of enforcement: by legal action through a court or by 'peer-group review'. By peer-group review, I mean a system by which a committee of expert individuals elected or nominated by governments monitors implementation. These experts usually serve in their personal capacity rather than as representatives of their governments. Governments are required to submit reports on how they are implementing the provisions of the instrument, and individual complaints are sometimes permitted. The experts usually have the power to examine representatives of governments on the reports and complaints submitted, to receive information from non-governmental organizations or others, and to present and publish reports on their findings. The details of these arrangements vary from one instrument to another. Only the EHR and its Protocols, and some provisions of the OAS Charter, as amended, and the AMR are enforced by courts. All the other provisions are enforced by peer-group review. I shall illustrate these two methods by giving a brief example of peer-review and by discussing the EHR at greater length.

The United Nations Human Rights Committee is the enforcement body for the ICPR under a system of peer-group review. A case concerning the right to education and scholastic freedom was raised, by Finnish atheists, who wished to secure for their children exemption from religious education.[3] The Committee's intervention led to a revision of Finnish legislation and guidance to teachers on teaching ethics and the history of religions.

The EHR has an elaborate procedure by which applications under the Convention are examined first by the Commission, and then by the EUCT or the Council of Ministers and sometimes by both. The decisions are binding on governments, but are scarcely enforceable. Governments normally comply with the decisions of the Court and amend legislation and procedures accordingly;

they may also be required to pay compensation to individuals who bring successful applications. Applications may be brought only after domestic remedies have been exhausted. The process is very slow, some cases taking six years or more. For all its limitations, the procedures under the EHR have been important in improving the law relating to issues of human rights in a number of countries.

Several decisions have concerned freedom of expression, a few the right to education, but none has dealt with academic freedom in higher education, although principles relevant to academic freedom have been established. For example in *Sunday Times* v. *United Kingdom* (Case No. 6538/74, Judgement: 2 EHRR, 245), the case about the banning of an article in the *Sunday Times* on the Thalidomide Affair, the Court had to decide whether the permitted limitations on freedom of expression covered the way in which the English courts had applied the rule governing contempt of court. The EUCT observed, following a previous judgement (*Handyside* v. *United Kingdom* 1975, 1 EHRR 737, the *Little Red School Book*) that freedom of expression:

> is applicable not only to information or ideas that are favourably received or regarded as inoffensive or as a matter of indifference, but also to those that offend, shock or disturb the State or any sector of the population.
>
> Brownlie 1981, p. 296

and

> Article 10 guarantees not only the freedom of the press to inform the public but also the right of the public to be properly informed.
>
> Brownlie 1981, p. 297

I can see no reason why these rights should not apply equally to universities and other educational establishments (and indeed to local authorities, despite the Local Government Act 1986), as well as to individuals and the Press, and thus cover aspects of academic freedom relating to publishing, research, teaching and learning.

The right to education has several times been held to be the right of an individual or of a child to the educational services already provided. Recent important cases with relevance for academic freedom have concerned compulsory sex education in Danish schools (*Kjeldsen, Busk Madsen and Pedersen* v. *Denmark*, Judgement, 7 December 1976, Series A, No. 23, 1 EHRR 711) and corporal punishment in Scottish schools (*Campbell and Cosans* v. *United Kingdom* Judgement, 25 February 1982, 3 *HRLJ*, 1982, No. 1–4, pp. 221–36), in both cases contrary to the parents' wishes. The judgement in the Danish case is important for its statement on the content of the curriculum. This states that care must be taken to ensure that:

> . . . information or knowledge included in the curriculum is conveyed in an objective, critical and pluralistic manner. The State is forbidden to pursue an aim of indoctrination that might be considered as not respecting parents' religious and philosophic convictions.
>
> (para. 36)

The Court explained what was meant by philosophic convictions in *Campbell and Cosans*: 'such convictions as are worthy of respect in a democratic society and not incompatible with human dignity' (para. 63). It held furthermore that the right to education is that of the child and dominates the rights of the parents and their convictions (see Rendel 1987).

These two judgements support the right to teach a range of views and opinions and indicate the type of views that will not be protected. The latter would presumably include racist, sexist and comparably derogatory views of, for example, disabled people, homosexuals or lesbians, as being incompatible with the human dignity of such persons.

Applying human rights principles

Academic freedom for the individual depends both on the institution and on the general rules operating in society. Academic freedom for the institution depends on the formal and informal rules governing its existence and on the resources available. Subject to these constraints, it is the most senior members of institutions who decide on policies and make many important individual decisions. Academic freedom can be limited from within academia as well as from outside, and such restrictions can apply both to knowledge itself and to individuals. Within academia conflicts will inevitably arise on the evaluation of research, teaching and students' work, on proper conduct and broadly disciplinary questions. Conflicts may arise between academia and the political, economic and cultural structures of society over the content and methods of teaching and research, the uses to which resources are put and the ownership of the products of research. How far can human rights principles and processes clarify and resolve such conflicts?

Human rights provisions are couched in individual terms aimed at protecting individuals from the State, but many writers base their claim for academic freedom on institutional autonomy. Institutional autonomy is no guarantee of individual academic freedom for academics, researchers or students, since institutions may treat individuals unfairly or with bias or prejudice. It has been suggested that either could exist without the other (Tight 1985, p. 21). However, it is difficult to see how individual academic freedom could exist without institutional autonomy, except for individual researchers working in libraries. Otherwise arrangements for individual scholars or groups of scholars would have to be made directly with the state or through academic professional associations, and institutions would be obliged to provide for the scholars – a system more theoretical than real. In practice, the academic freedom of the individual depends on institutional autonomy. Institutional autonomy is a necessary but not a sufficient condition of academic freedom.

The means of protecting individuals against unfair treatment by the institution lie first in internal procedures and then in national law. Human rights documents are mostly silent on security of tenure in employment, protection against unfair dismissal and the rights of students. They do, however, seek to protect the right to collective bargaining, which should contribute to fair treatment, and to joint consultation, but the latter is not the same as the participation in the government of the institution which academic staff expect. The gaps are compounded by the lack of an agreed code of conduct and practice binding on academics.

The *Lernfreiheit* of students, who can be seen as clients of academia, depends largely on careful and conscientious teaching, and integrity in examining. Does their academic freedom also require individual attention, counselling and other support services and facilities, crêches, nurseries, hostels, refectories, sports-fields, health services and so on? Such services and facilities can increase opportunities for students from disadvantaged groups and so increase their academic freedom. What rights have students in relation to the content and structure of the curriculum, the forms of assessment and examination? These issues, so prominent in 1968, led to at least a small and temporary shift in power away from senior academic staff to students. Some, for example Ions (1970), saw the participation of students in the decision-making processes of higher education, including the content of the curriculum and methods of teaching, as a threat to academic freedom. Since students are transitory and staff more permanent, it seems unlikely that students' participation could pose a permanent threat to the academic freedom of academic staff.

More recently, the hostility of students at Ruskin College, the trade union college at Oxford, towards David Selbourne because he published an article in *The Times* when that paper was in dispute with the unions arose from the conflict between the students' view of trade union solidarity and Selbourne's freedom of expression (e.g. Hirst 1986). In Britain at least, students' activism has led to hostility to higher education as well as to students themselves, since the institutions and their teaching have been blamed for the students' behaviour. Indeed, onerous duties have now been laid on institutions of higher education and their staff by Section 43 of the Education (No. 2) Act 1986 to ensure that freedom of speech within the law is assured to staff, students and visiting speakers. This Section was enacted because extreme right-wing speakers and some Conservative ministers had been shouted down by students at meetings to which they had been invited by other students.

Conflicts arising from the evaluation of academic work cause particular difficulties because academic institutions are in effect licensing bodies, both for persons and for knowledge. They license persons directly by awarding degrees and diplomas to those who have met approved standards of knowledge and intellectual skills. This license is an essential prerequisite for many professions and other influential and, ultimately, powerful occupations. For this reason, academics are able to influence the future leaders of a very large range of activities, including future teachers who will in turn influence future citizens. Academics carry out these functions through their own teaching, the official curricula they devise, the examinations they set, the hidden curricula they support, the books and articles they recommend and the standards they require to be met. They license more indirectly through their influence over the examinations set by other examining bodies (and are sometimes influenced by them), by their advice to publishers on the manuscripts of books, by expert advice to government and to other official bodies, by participation in the media and by other extra-mural activities. Such influence over content is also a means of licensing or legitimating particular forms and blocks of knowledge. What is taught or published is licensed, legitimated or official knowledge. What is omitted is not. These licensing activities are important public functions, although academics have no monopoly of them. They are part of the *raison d'être* of academia and in exercising them academics may contribute to maintaining or challenging the hegemony that legitimates the existing social order.

However, despite their function of sponsoring intellectual development and innovation, institutions of higher education have not always been willing to recognize the scholarly value of new (or even old) ideas, interpretations or disciplines. Marxism, especially in the United States, labour history, trade union studies, Black Studies and Women's Studies have all suffered obstruction. This is scarcely surprising since academia may be seen by some as part of the ideological apparatus of the State, the modern replacement of the Church, with the duty of maintaining the orthodox social order, of keeping speculation within bounds, and of upholding loyalty to the State. Consequently new ideas, interpretations and disciplines that challenge orthodoxies are likely to be obstructed.

The opposition to Women's Studies (which have developed in Britain since the mid-1970s) can be seen in this light. Not only do the new knowledge and understanding presented by feminist scholars pose a threat to the patriarchal order, but this new knowledge is taught overwhelmingly by women scholars, members of a subordinated group, and especially responds to the needs and demands of women students, a group whose abilities and commitment have been substantially underestimated. Furthermore, the feminist critique has wide-ranging implications for much of legitimated knowledge, for research methods and for methods of teaching. The feminist critique also raises major political questions relating to the values of society and the expression of those values in hierarchy, dominance, aggression, exploitation and inequality. What is surprising is not that Women's Studies should have been opposed, but that the opposition has not been more severe. This relative success could be attributed generously to the values, and willingness to act on those values, of a significant proportion of senior academics or, more cynically, to the discovery, in times of financial need, that Women's Studies attract students and to the reassurance given by the obvious commitment and high standards of both the students and the staff engaged in such courses.

If we apply the principles set out in the three human rights cases discussed earlier to the problem of the legitimation of knowledge and ideas it is clear that academia would be under an obligation to include within the curriculum a range of ideas and information reflecting religious and philosophical convictions that are not incompatible with human dignity. It would not matter that the State or any section of the population was offended, shocked or disturbed by this teaching. The public, including the students and other clients of academia, would be entitled to be properly informed. Both *Lehrfreiheit* and *Lernfreiheit* would be safeguarded. These arguments could be applied equally to research. By the same arguments and principles, academia could defend itself from attack.

It might be more difficult to use these principles to insert new ideas, interpretations and disciplines. In such cases, the Court would have to be persuaded that the new material was academically worthy. But the best evidence of academic worthiness would have to come from the academic establishment. This very requirement would, however, help to protect controversial subject-matter, such as Women's Studies, Marxist, anti-sexist and anti-racist teaching and practice, that had already been accepted within the curriculum.

The provisions of the EHR and the principles established by judgements could, I suggest, contribute to protecting at least some of the ingredients of academic freedom, and in particular the content of teaching and research, from direct restrictions. It is also clear that individuals would be able to claim their freedom of expression as individuals, but not necessarily as academics. That is, they could say what they liked as individuals but could not necessarily teach what they liked, if, for example, a State refused to fund the teaching of certain subjects or topics. This freedom, like *Lernfreiheit*, depends on institutional autonomy and the commitment of institutions to academic freedom.

Academia, society and the state

Academia, in addition to its right and duty to seek truth and to teach, has obligations to society to train individuals for jobs and to provide useful research results. These rights, duties and obligations often conflict and such conflicts are systemic and probably inevitable.

Conflicts may arise between academia and its clients who wish to employ graduates and to obtain the research knowledge that academics produce. The employer often lacks the knowledge, or may have too narrow a vision, to perceive what education and training are needed for an efficient labour force; indeed, the employer's concepts of labour relations and managerial prerogative may militate against an effective use of staff. In a comparable way, those commissioning research may not be able to formulate appropriate questions for researchers to answer, may not have the knowledge necessary to elicit research to answer their problems or may want answers only within their own frame of reference (which may itself be mistaken or at least open to doubt). Such criticisms have been raised against the customer–contractor principle in research (Lord Privy Seal 1971). These are the very questions which academics have, or should have, the specific expertise to answer since an essential part of the academic's job is to relate theories to general statements about society, processes of work and of change, and to specific events and practices; in other words to relate levels of generality and of specificity to each other. Hence customers, by trying to specify too precisely what they want, are wasting much of the ability of academics, both teachers and researchers. Indeed the very word 'customer' is misleading. Shops have customers, professionals have clients or patients.

In relation to both teaching and research, academic freedom is necessary as a benefit for clients and society generally. The Study Group on Scholarly Freedom argued that, as professionals, academics need academic freedom because others may suffer if academics are denied the right to practise their professions (1977, para. 3.6.3, p. 29). They argued for a professional freedom akin to the clinical freedom accorded to the medical profession. The Group based their claim on Article 29(i) of the UDHR (*ibid.*, para. 3.6.6, p. 29): 'Everyone has duties to the community in which alone the free and full development of his (sic) personality is possible'.

Interference in the process of disseminating the results of scientific research, and providing the opportunity for others to test and confirm, correct or refute the results, all of which are aspects of academic freedom, could, the Group argued, produce 'bad' science. Lysenkoism perhaps most vividly illustrates this point. Scientific research can, however, produce dangerous and threatening inventions, such as atom bombs. The Study Group, specifically concerned with the natural sciences, made clear that they did not hold 'to the oversimplified ethical view that the pursuit of knowledge transcends all moral or legal constraints' (*ibid.*, para. 2.4.4, p. 17).

Instead, they said, serious consideration must be given to the grounds for restricting scientific freedom.

Academia has varied and often conflicting rights, duties and obligations and many clients whose interests conflict with each other. The difficulties arising from these conflicts are compounded by the dependence of all systems of higher education on public funding. Individual universities may be able to survive and even flourish without direct government funding, but probably they all benefit in some way from indirect government funding, through relief from certain taxes and through tax benefits attached to donations.

It is scarcely surprising that academia has been subject to attack. These attacks are of three main kinds: ideological, managerial and financial.

Ideological attacks

Ideological attacks on academic freedom are not new; they date back at least to Socrates in 400 B.C. They occur under all types of regime, from communist to liberal democratic, as the *Berufsverbot* in the Federal Republic of Germany, and the witchhunts of the 1950s and 1960s in the United States show. The intellectual quality of the attacks is often poor and in Britain, at least, direct ideological attacks have not so far had much success. Such attacks are clearly contrary to the principles enunciated in the judgements of the EUCT and in the Convention itself. In the long run attacks often fail – Plato's accounts of Socrates' views are still basic texts – but they can be exceedingly troublesome and dangerous in the short run. The repression of, for example, Marxist interpretations means that serious critiques of such interpretations cannot be made, hence increasing the possibility of such interpretations being surreptitiously and uncritically adopted. Nor does one have to be a Marxist or a feminist to recognize the value of such interpretations in compelling a critical scrutiny and informed understanding of existing society. A further undesirable consequence of ideological attacks is that scholars and researchers impose a self-censorship. Even if thought ranges freely, expression does not.

Managerial attacks

Managerial attacks seek to impose on academic institutions procedures for making decisions and managing staff and resources similar to those in commercial businesses. In addition to being an attack on institutional autonomy, and through that on individual academic freedom, this analogy ignores the complex, specialized and often contradictory nature of the tasks undertaken by academic institutions, and the very considerable conceptual and practical difficulties of measuring and quantifying success. The full benefit of higher education is not measurable either by the individual, by the employer or society even though graduates' greater lifetime earnings can be quantified.

Financial attacks

At least as serious now are the financial attacks, which seem aimed more at securing government control of academia then at moderating the cost of increasing demand. In Britain these attacks range across the entire spectrum of academic work and include medical, agricultural and other scientific research as well as social sciences and humanities. Neither students' ability to pay fees, nor the generosity of benefactors, nor the self-interest of sponsors can compensate for the loss of public funds.

The effect of financial cuts has been to restrict the development of new courses and activities, to reduce the length and content of courses, to lower standards of teaching and provision, especially of books and journals in libraries, to reduce the mobility of staff and to reduce the number of individuals with access to higher education (Kloss 1985, Gellert 1985). Hence the *Lernfreiheit* of students as well as the *Lehrfreiheit* of staff is being reduced. The oblique attack is the more dangerous in that it is being presented both as an opportunity for making better use of resources, providing greater choice(!) and courses of more relevance to the economy of the country, and to the needs of employers and individuals.

Defending academic freedom

How far can human rights provisions protect academic freedom against ideological, managerial or financial attacks? Human rights instruments are of little or no avail in the United States, as that government has ratified few of them. The United Kingdom has ratified many, though not all. As we have seen, human rights provisions do offer some protection against ideological attack. Can they be applied against managerial and financial attacks that have a veiled ideological purpose?

There are, as far as I know, no legal, constitutional or human rights provisions which require non-discrimination in relation to different academic subjects. However, it is well-documented that the proportions of men and women in different subjects are very unequal. Substantially reducing the number of places and the amount of teaching in some subjects might constitute indirect discrimination on grounds of sex. We can only speculate whether a case based on such an argument could be developed successfully either in the British courts (probably not) or in the European Court of Justice (ECJ) or in the EUCT, and used to protect social sciences and humanities for academics and for students. If such a case were successful in the ECJ, we should benefit from the strong enforcement powers of the European Community.

A broader and more direct approach would depend on being able to prove that the cuts in the funding of higher education, and the ways in which they were implemented, were in fact an infringement of the freedom of expression of academics and students and of the right to education of students. Such a line of argument would be difficult to sustain, but perhaps not wholly impossible.

Legal remedies are slow, costly and uncertain. Political remedies based on traditional civil and political human rights, many of them enacted in national and in constitutional laws as well as in instruments of human rights, may be quicker and as effective. In western democracies such remedies would obviously include publicity, lobbying, pressure on the legislature, on politicians and so on. Such activities contribute also to creating and maintaining a public consciousness in favour of academic freedom. The problem for Britain is that the *only* superordinate legislation is the EHR and that of the EEC.

Academics in one country can help those in another. The Study Group on Scholarly Freedom discussed ways of showing solidarity with oppressed scientists which included visiting such scientists in their countries, applying private pressure (not very effective they thought) or public pressure (which they found to be of more use). They discussed the merits and demerits of refusing scholarly papers from oppressing countries (not helpful) or of refusing to hold conferences in them (useful paras 5.4 and 5.5, pp. 56–59). These recommendations assume that the scholars taking action are working in countries where academic freedom does exist.

Towards a convention on academic freedom

Existing human rights documents do not provide adequately for academic freedom. A Charter drawn up by academics as a way of preparing for a Declaration and a subsequent Convention on Academic Freedom is needed. The discussion that such a project could engender would make both specialized publics and the general public more aware of the benefits that higher education can confer on society as a whole as well as on individuals, and of the conditions necessary for academia to carry out these functions. Such a debate would be more productive than a defence of what look, to some outsiders, like unaccountable vested interests.

Such a Charter should clearly lay on institutions of higher education and on all their staff not only a right but a duty to defend academic freedom by ensuring that they teach a plurality of interpretations and material within a framework supportive of human dignity. In the context of existing instruments, as indicated earlier, human dignity must mean equality and non-discrimination. In order to assist academics and researchers in their work and in the execution of their public functions, a code of professional conduct and practice needs to be drawn up. This should include rights and obligations in relation to publication of research, the treatment of students and staff, procedures for appointment, probation, promotion, dismissal and so on. In return, tenure in the traditional sense, subject to proper safeguards, should exist to protect the individual academic, teacher or researcher from unjust treatment by the institution, its governing body, the State or others.

The attack on tenure in Britain in part results from the elitism and exclusiveness of British education, the ease with which tenure has been granted in the past, the over-generous and unduly tolerant treatment of some staff, the unfair treatment of others and the sheer incompetence of some institutions in dealing with some staffing matters. Tenure is important because it can defend not only the individual academic but also the institution from ideological and managerial pressures, by helping them to continue to teach unfashionable or unpopular subjects, to research inconvenient topics and to provide more centres of initiative than hierarchical management can. For these reasons, institutions need tenure for individuals in order to protect their own autonomy.

For institutional autonomy, financial sufficiency is also required. This is more difficult to achieve and requires that the State is either willing or feels obliged to fund those who may be publicly critical of it. Human rights instruments provide some institutional support for academic freedom, but the State will not provide for it unless the people love truth and freedom.

Notes

1 Lionel Robbins is one of those who lay most stress on institutional autonomy, especially in the Robbins Report (Committee on Higher Education 1963, chapter 16). Other statements of academic freedom which I have consulted include Arblaster 1974, AUT 1974, Griffith *et al.* 1972, Kaplan and Schrecker 1983, NUS/NCCL 1970, Pincoffs 1975, Robbins 1966, Schrecker 1986, Study Group on Scholarly Freedom 1977, Tight 1985. I found the articles in Kaplan & Schrecker especially helpful.

2 Incumbents of the Church of England and judges enjoy tenure subject to good behaviour or absence of serious misconduct. In practice other groups of workers enjoy something akin to tenure in that it is very difficult to dismiss them without 'good cause' or because of other peculiarities in their contracts.

3 *Hartikainen and others* v. *Finland*, Communication No. R9/40, 30 September 1978, Report of the UN Human Rights Committee, Vol. A/36/40, 1981, pp. 147–152, and Vol. A/38/40, 1983, pp. 255–6.

8

Limits to Academic Freedom: Imposed-Upon or Self-Imposed?

Ronald Barnett

Preliminaries

Higher education is a pivotal institution in modern society. It is also a key part of the total apparatus of the state. Not only in the United Kingdom and in other countries where the state directly contributes the dominant portion of the costs of the enterprise, but even in the United States, higher education is required to provide services to the economy in its widest sense. The attention now being given in the United Kingdom to employment rates and patterns of graduate destinations is simply a manifestation of the taken-for-granted expectation that institutions of higher education should mesh with those of the wider society. In the field of research, again, society exerts its claims on a higher education system which is apparently happy to accept society's monies, and not only in the spheres of military or heavy-cost civil research. It is not just economic connections that are apparent: a wide range of interconnections between higher education and the social fabric (to be outlined later) can also be readily identified.

In short, higher education in the modern world is inescapably bound into its host society. If the term 'academic freedom' ever implied the desirability for the academic community to separate itself off from the wider society, that kind of aspiration must today be seen for the nonsense it is.

It is a nonsense both sociologically and philosophically. Sociologically there simply can be no opting out for higher education. It is a social institution not only *in* society but *of* society. To add to the examples above, we need only observe the attention given to 'access' to higher education: if it is not yet seen as a general right, in practice many sections of the professional and managerial classes have come to see admission to higher education as a right for their offspring (Edwards 1982, p. 105). Against the background of nearly one thousand years of history, this widespread commitment to and claim upon higher education is a recent phenomenon. Equally, it is a set of claims that higher education for the most part has willingly undertaken to meet. Whether this situation is best described as one of 'accommodation' of higher education to the modern industrial state (Galbraith 1969, p. 372), or whether we see it as higher education 'serving' society, the result is the same: there can be no uncoupling of higher education, as social institution, from the rest of society. Or at least, no such uncoupling is even remotely in sight.

If the idea of academic freedom as a bid for independence is a sociological nonsense, it is also a philosophical nonsense. And it is so on two grounds.

First, the idea signifies an epistemological naivety. Higher education, whether in its research or teaching functions, deals in knowledge. That is its currency. But knowledge is also a currency of modern society itself. The edifices of knowledge that are created within higher education are not hermetically sealed from what passes for knowledge in society. There is trade and movement in both directions. The 'knowledge industry' of higher education not only takes many of its problems, research priorities and cognitive resources from society; whether in the 'hard' sciences or the softer humanities, higher education also acts surreptitiously to legitimate society's cognitive structure. Witchcraft and astrology are out; quarks and computers are in. Despite the views of those who claim to see a sharp break between the knowledge on offer in higher education and society, in an age when virtually everyone is linguistically literate (Gellner 1964) and many are computer-literate (if only in reading their shopping bill), the epistemological currency of higher education and society run into each other.

Secondly, there is, in some readings of the notion of academic freedom, a kind of moral supremacy to be claimed and secured by the academic community against its host society. But such a view contains a misreading of the language of morals represented by those two spheres of human interaction. Certainly, the academic community has its own standards of excellence 'which are appropriate to, and partially definitive of, that form of activity' (MacIntyre 1985, p. 187). But then so do other spheres of activity to be found in society. In MacIntyre's terminology, chess no less than chemistry, painting no less than physics, politics no less than political science, are all examples of 'practices', with their own intrinsic worth, offering unending opportunities for human endeavour and creativity (or 'virtue') according to particular standards and values.

At the same time, being an institution *of* its host society, higher education is also subject to the dominant values of that society. And so we see, in the language of performance indicators (Committee of Vice-Chancellors and Principals (CVCP 1987)), of 'good management' (CVCP 1985; National Advisory Body (NAB) 1987) and of first destination statistics, the signs that higher education is being breached by the means–end thinking characteristic of the wider society.

In short, in terms of its inner set of ethics, there can be no easy assumption of higher education resting on a code of morality separate from and purer than that of society.

What do these opening reflections amount to? Simply this: if, under the idea of academic freedom, there lurks the image of the ivory tower, then both the idea and the associated imagery need major overhaul. Higher education cannot claim, if indeed it ever could or wanted to, that position of purity in relation to the wider society (cf. Gellner 1969, p. 105). Indeed, higher education now takes in the washing of its host society. It can do no other, even if it so wanted.

It follows that any attempt to work out a modern idea of academic freedom has to be sensitive and adequate to this necessary integration of higher education into the culture (in the widest sense) of society. That is to say, the modern idea of academic freedom has to recognize the presence of society not simply as an irritation to be circumvented but rather, in significant senses, as constitutive of higher education itself.

What is required, then, is nothing short of a theory of academic freedom which does justice to the actual relationship between higher education and society rather than an imaginary relationship. To inject some alternative imagery, that relationship is not so much one of mutual wariness (like boxers sizing up each other) as of intertwined structures (like a double helix), each part of which is distinct though bound up in the other and interacting on various levels. In this situation, higher education cannot opt out of society; it cannot pretend to a position of social and cognitive purity, for it is simply not available. 'Academic freedom' has, therefore, as a symbol of claimed and supposed separateness of the academic community from society, to stand in the dock accused of being the self-serving rhetoric of an interest group, having little purchase on the sociological and philosophical realities of the modern higher education system in society today.

The principle of academic freedom

Accordingly, we need to start by asking if, given this situation, the idea of academic freedom serves any real – as opposed to rhetorical – purpose at all. Is it more than an attempt by a small, though not unimportant, community to carve out special privileges for itself?

One way of pursuing the issue could lie in recalling that the origin of the idea of academic freedom actually lay in a recognition that society had *legitimate* interests in higher education, and that some means was required to demarcate those interests from those of the members of the academic community itself. 'Academic freedom' served, therefore, to mark the boundaries of society's legitimate interest in the affairs of the community. It was a way of identifying certain activities of the academic community as being beyond the scope of the legitimate interests of society. To put it crudely, the taxpayer had rights in relation to the increasingly expensive system of higher education, but those rights ended at the interface with higher education. Satisfaction could be sought in relation to access for would-be students, in relation to the balance-sheet or the management of the institution's finances, and in relation to the economic and social opportunities which a higher education conferred on its graduates. But the internal activities were assumed to be a matter for the academic community.

The model was probably always mythical, but it served its purpose for a time. Ultimately, though, it lost all pretence at offering a faithful account of the higher education–society relationship. But, before we abandon it altogether and attempt to put something else in its place, what did the traditional model of academic freedom amount to? It may have rested on a particular theory of knowledge, and a set of values in relation to academic activities (Searle, 1972, p. 172), but it was in essence quite simple. It can be expressed in the form of a single principle: *that academic pursuits, carried out in academic settings, by academic persons, should be ultimately directed by those academic persons.*

Certainly, questions can be raised about each of these terms. For example, does the keeping of animals for the purpose of experiments count as an academic pursuit? Or is the writing of an article in a newspaper (that is, outside the range of the recognizably academic literature) an academic pursuit? Does the television studio count as an academic setting, if it is not under the control of the Open University? Does the scholar's favourite armchair count as an academic setting, even if it is in the home? Do students count as academic persons? Or does the politician in giving a lecture on campus count as an academic person?

All of these are real questions, since they bear upon practical issues raised under the banner of academic freedom; and they deserve some kind of answer. Or, at least, a theory of academic freedom has to show that it is not speechless in the face of such practical questions. Unless it can, the theory would be merely cant.

I believe that the general principle just set out could be unpacked so as to offer some guidance on practical questions, where academic freedom is invoked. Definitive answers, however, will not be forthcoming (Brown 1973). This is because additional assumptions and values would need to be brought in, which would themselves be debatable.

For example, it could be argued that the role of the student, while not fully an academic role (not carrying the responsibilities and demands of that role), is nevertheless a quasi-academic role. At its best, the activities of the student, in effect, constitute those of a kind of shadow academic, in terms of the attention to detail, the independence of thought, the presentation of work and so forth. Consequently, on this view, students are entitled to some measure of academic freedom (Magsino 1978). Correspondingly, the politician on the campus is neither an academic nor engaged in academic pursuits, and so is not entitled to claim the right to 'academic freedom'; though the same politician might well be entitled to claim general civil rights.

But these views are just that. We arrive at them by adding in to the general principle other premises or values. The view about the student, for instance, rests on the premiss that the student does actually take a quasi-academic role, rather than being a passive recipient of an imposed curriculum. It also relies on the implicit value that students, while not being full academics in their formal role, nevertheless deserve to be so treated, if only in part.

But, to return to the general point being made here, to get into this debate is itself to miss the point. For however useful such a principle as that offered earlier might seem, however conceptually powerful its attractions in helping us to 'place' our problems (even if not answering them), it is, in the end, *beside* the point.

Incorporation reemphasized

A general abstract principle of academic freedom is bound to fail to do justice to the complexities of the higher education–society relationship within the modern state. Some of the ways in which higher education is incorporated into the modern state have been mentioned and it has been indicated that higher education is by no means an unwilling partner in many aspects of that incorporation. For that incorporation has provided for the expansion of the higher education system, and, with that expansion, an infusion of resources of an extraordinary kind (at least, when viewed against a period only a generation ago). That expansion, in student numbers, personnel, research activity, institutions, and support staff, means that higher education is big business (amounting to some four billion pounds annually in the United Kingdom). But more than that, that expansion alone, underwritten as it is by the state, signifies the legitimation of higher education as a crucial institution *of* the modern state.

Underlying these admittedly abstract observations can be identified a variety of ways in which the internal life of institutions of higher education reflects the interests of the wider society.

Curriculum

First of all, the curriculum itself is increasingly influenced by considerations of economic utility. This is particularly evident in the design of courses in which professional bodies have an interest; there are, in the polytechnic and colleges sector alone, about ninety such professional bodies. Professional bodies are in a particularly strong position in relation to course design where they formally 'accredit' courses. Graduation on an accredited degree course may, in some instances, be the only route into a profession; or it may offer exemption from the whole or a significant part of the professional body's own professional examinations (Brennan, 1981).

But quite apart from particular cases of this sort, there is a much more general awareness of the link between graduation and the student's employability. The link is emphasized by governments in justifying their expenditures on higher education, and it is reinforced inevitably by employers of graduates. Their attitudes are admittedly not always consistent. On the one hand, specialized knowledge and expertise are sought (Secretary of State of Education, 1987); on the other hand, it is transferable skills that are said to be important (e.g. NAB, 1986). Nevertheless, the sense that courses in higher education, whatever the subject area, ought to generate opportunities for their graduates to enter the labour market is generally accepted by the academic community itself. Students' 'first destination' statistics commonly figure amongst performance data on courses, and the academic community is questioning itself on ways of making its courses, even (or especially) in the humanities, more attractive to commerce and industry.

In short, not only is the wider world no longer outside the system of higher education: it has entered significantly into one of the central activities of its internal life.

Research

But the curriculum, and with it the student experience, is not the only area to be affected by these currents. The other dominant academic activity, that of research, has also been subject to them. First, 'applied research' and now 'strategic research' grow in scale relative to 'pure research', so that the space available for pure research is diminishing. The major research funding agencies attempt to rationalize their work by identifying major problem areas, whether in industrial, economic or social spheres, which require a concerted research attack. In the jargon, the funding bodies have become 'proactive' rather than merely responsive. Further consequences have been that the areas in which major grants are distributed have diminished, and the numbers of individual academics who can realistically hope to share in any significant way in their distribution have also shrunk, as the monies go to favoured ('selected') research groups. As the output of the favoured groups grows, so they become even more attractive to the funding bodies; and those outside the charmed circles can only look on.

Again, it has to be recalled that, despite the frequent plaintive cries about the system, it is one in which the academic community is largely acquiescing. Even its complaints are about the operation of the system ('insufficient funds for grade A bids') rather than about the fundamentals of the system itself.

What is the upshot of these observations, admittedly at a somewhat administrative level, for our concerns with academic freedom? Simply this: in both teaching and research, the available space for members of the academic community freely to determine the shape and direction of their own activities is increasingly limited. Indeed, it has so shrunk as to have almost vanished. In one sense, of course, that is why academic freedom is so problematic, and is on the agenda today. But the point being made here is that higher education is now so inseparably part of the state, that there can be no going back.

Willing partners

In fact, much of the angst now being registered by the academic community actually has the whiff of sour grapes about it. For, as remarked, the position in which higher education in the United Kingdom now finds itself is the inevitable outcome of the academic community's willingness over the last thirty years to subscribe to an increasing involvement by the state in higher education. That path offered opportunities for resources and status not otherwise available. The intermeshing of higher education into the wider society is not the result of one partner being dragged totally unwillingly into the new relationship: it was a development in which both entered shaking hands, as it were, if not actually embracing each other. The result is that the close interweaving between higher education and the rest of society is inseparably part of our modern conception of higher education.

It could hardly be otherwise. And, to repeat, the interconnections take place not just at the fringes, in terms of additional resources being made available from commercial or industrial firms, or through the employment avenues of graduates. The interconnections are at work right in the heart of the academic community itself. It is not just that some academics may be, in effect, salesmen for computer or electronics companies, 'advising' the students and their fellow academics on their private purchases of calculators or word-processors; or that the odd tailor-made full-cost course may be provided to an industry; or that professorial chairs are being endowed by private corporations. It is, as stated, that the interests of the wider society enter the teaching and research activities in the mainstream of the internal life of our institutions of higher education.

This interlocking of higher education and the modern society – as distinct from the servicing role that the system has provided ever since its mediaeval origins – is relatively recent and has amounted to a silent revolution in the inner (and largely hidden) workings of our institutions. Given the centrality of higher education in the modern state, it could be no other way. Higher education has become too important to leave to the academics; and the academics largely understand and accept this. The advantages are more than mere fringe benefits.

I have so far drawn attention to professional, industrial, social, economic, financial and managerial interests of the wider society which are at work within, and through, the individual members of the academic community. This, though, by no means exhausts the influences which bear upon the academic community. There are others which are even less obvious, but are (partly for that reason) more influential. I have in mind cultural and ideological dimensions of our institutions of higher education. We can only lightly touch on some aspects here.

The cultural dimension

The writings of the French sociologist, Pierre Bourdieu, make it clear that higher education confers not just economic capital on successful graduates, but cultural capital as well (e.g. Bourdieu and Passeron 1979). One way of putting this is simply to recall that, despite their formal equivalence, a degree in subject X gained at Oxbridge provides a greater range of life chances than a degree in the same subject gained at a local institute of higher education. Indeed, a third class degree from Oxbridge may count for more than a first class degree from an institute of higher education. The point is made easily enough, but in fact it reflects the profound and subtle ways in which higher education is part of the culture, in its general sense, of society. The connections between different kinds of institution of higher education and different strata or socio-economic groups sustain not a shared understanding of specialized knowledge fields, but a shared culture, in the sense of a linguistic and a social competence of a certain general character. Hoggart's scholarship grammar school working-class boy found entrance even to a red-brick university 'a leap out of the tradition' (Hoggart 1958, p. 294). On the other hand, the move from public school to Oxbridge would normally lead to very little trauma, for the implicit values and assumptions of the two communities resemble each other in large part. Parallel cultural linkages, though of a quite different kind, can be seen in some institutions in the public sector, which for instance are committed to attracting students from disadvantaged social groups of various kinds, and providing an appropriate educational milieu for them.

The ideological dimension

Ideology is a slippery term, but it represents a further dimension in which the wider society is implicated in the internal life of higher education. We have already touched on the new managerial ethos affecting institutions, and noted that the curriculum is turned towards the economy in a variety of ways. 'Economic determinism' is too strong a term to describe these tendencies, for they are more subtle than that. Rather they are representative of a larger and nebulous *Weltanschaung* which characterizes the wider society. It is, in short, an ideology, a general and widely sustained consciousness which is at the same time reflective of the dominant interests of a modern industrial society (Habermas, 1971). The continuing and increasing insistence on shifting the balance of courses in the direction of science and technology, the wide use of information technology, the establishment of teaching companies and science parks, the concern over intellectual property and patents and the marketing of higher education's services are all obvious enough manifestations of the syndrome.

But it operates at deeper levels, affecting the consciousness of the academic community in its research endeavours. The culture of the wider society, including its concepts, technological products, and dominant values, provides a rich source of metaphors and other cognitive resources on which scientific research draws (Barnes, 1974). The presence of computer models of the brain in psychology, the development of performance indicators in a health studies research unit, the research on the transistor (Gibbons and Johnson 1982) and even the framework of mathematical thought (Bloor 1976) are all examples.

Résumé

The general point made so far is actually quite straightforward. It is certainly possible and by no means useless to engage in a reflective inquiry on the meaning of academic freedom, its scope and its limits. Indeed, not only is it worthwhile: that kind of inquiry actually needs to be undertaken at periodic intervals. To pick up the terms of the formulation offered earlier, our notions of academic persons, academic settings and academic activities are all liable to undergo modification, and, therefore, are likely to affect the implementation of the general principle of academic freedom.

But such a theoretical exercise needs to be placed in a larger context. The context sketched out here is that of the interconnections between higher education and the wider society. Given the range, depth and intractability of the interconnections just glimpsed, it needs to be recognized that academic freedom cannot, in the modern society, represent some kind of *carte blanche* for members of the academic profession. The influences, pressures and indeed requirements are testimony to a different story.

But, as already intimated, it would be misleading to say simply that the scope of academic freedom is limited. For such a description might imply an arbitrary imposition upon the academic community from outside. Rather, on the account given here, what we have is both a more complicated and a more subtle situation. More complicated, because the academic community is, for the most part, compliant in the incorporation of higher education into the modern state (Rose and Rose, 1976, ch. 2). And more subtle, because that incorporation, precisely through having the assent of the academic community, is unnoticed by the academic community itself. In other words, the narrowing in the actual scope of academic freedom as it is exercised in practice is simply not normally apparent to the members of the academic community themselves, for they are willing accomplices in their own unfreedom.

Calls for the right to academic freedom, then, need to be seen as being voiced within a *taken-for-granted* social setting which has already put boundaries on the expression of academic freedom. Indeed, given the wholesale incorporation of higher education into the modern state, it is a matter of judgement how far a debate about academic freedom is a matter of the fine tuning of a vehicle, the shape, size, colour, status, engine and general individual and social benefit from which are unalterable. Again, though, to emphasize the point, in so far as these features of the vehicle are predetermined and not seriously discussable, it is in part because the driver and passengers are, for the most part, happy with the current state of affairs. They have been told they can have any colour they like, so long as it's black, and they are only too happy to accept black – particularly since the alternative is to walk.

Self-limitations to academic freedom

It will be rightly inferred from the foregoing argument that the compliant passengers include both teachers *and* students, but the point should perhaps be substantiated further for both groups.

The students

First, the students. Major empirical studies on changing student values have not recently been conducted, so mere hunch will have to serve. Accepting that the student body is heterogeneous (and more so now than ever), there appears to be a consensus amongst those close to higher education that the last ten to fifteen years have seen a marked change in the character of the general student outlook. Admittedly, the students of the radical movement and its aftermath in the late 1960s and early 1970s and the students of today both share a disinclination to be involved in the formal decision-making machinery of institutions of higher education. But the motivations at work are remarkable for their dissimilarities.

The students of the radical movement disavowed participation in the senate or academic board committees because it was irrelevant to their desire to see a wholesale transformation of the internal workings of academic institutions. From that perspective, any student acting in that role would have been hardly less than a 'collaborator' with the opposition, assisting in sustaining a non-democratic form of institutional politics. In contrast, today's students are reluctant to become involved in the minutiae of internal government because it is seen as marginal to their own individual interests. And those interests lie simply in the individuals' endeavours to secure, from student days, the greatest subsequent economic return.

Certainly, the radical student movement not merely represented a grave threat to academic freedom; it actually had that effect in many ways (Hook, 1970). Academic staff were prevented from going about their legitimate affairs, very often through actual physical assaults, or verbal assaults that were hardly less serious. But how should we characterize the present student mood? The academic freedom of staff is no longer (or only very rarely) at issue. But what of the students' own 'academic freedom' – their right, not to teach and research, but to learn (*Lernfreiheit*)?

One might have speculated, as the prospects of secure and prized forms of employment following graduation day are no longer assured, that students would turn to expressing their right to effective teaching, and a learning experience that would make a good class of degree more likely. Students might have sensed that the right to learn is made real partly through a recognition by institutions of higher education that they have a responsibility towards providing a positive learning experience. In other words, there might have been a widespread demand from students that the academic community look to improving teaching effectiveness and the quality of the student experience. On the contrary, however: students now seem to believe that their destiny with the external examiners lies entirely in their own hands. Consequently, modern students appear to be essentially 'alone', focused instrumentally on the final outcome, relatively passive imbibers of what is placed before them, undemanding, undemonstrative, and narrow in their conception of the place of their studies in wider education (is the idea of a higher education as offering a broad education, achieved through reading round and beyond one's subject and through long conversations with students from many other disciplines, entirely a romantic vision of the past?).

In short, students of today, in this society, have an impoverished conception of their own rights to academic freedom. There is no problem of student academic freedom today because the student body has itself drawn in its sense of the student role. Students are acquiescent in the learning and institutional experience that comes their way not because it is imposed upon them, but because of the stance they have themselves taken up. The student's right to learn is not seen as a problem of academic freedom because it is not seen as a problem at all. And it is not seen as a problem because the contraction in the student role, and consequently in the expression of the student's rights, is self-imposed.

Threats to academic freedom can, then, be self-imposed just as much as they can be imposed from outside. The self-imposed threats are, in actuality, more dangerous, because being self-imposed, they are unnoticed. They are insidious; their opaqueness makes them more difficult to confront, for that invisibility is testimony to their being underwritten by the groups involved.

The teachers

A parallel situation is present within the fully paid-up members of the academic community. Here, too, we find an undue limitation in the role, a limitation which is reflected in the self-conception of the actors involved. For academics define themselves less as 'academics' *per se*, but as members of some sub-set of those historically comprising the academic community. The physicist; the legal educator; the lecturer in nursing studies; the philosopher; all of them see themselves primarily not as a member of the entire world of 'academics', but as a member of their own disciplinary profession.

The main consequence is obvious enough: there is today no academic community in any real sense of the term; it is just a matter of a series of groupings, admittedly all the time shifting their shape, with some being taken over by others, others seeking out allies in transdisciplinary groupings. The shifting sands of disciplinary politics emphasize the point. Not only is there a lack of community across academics; there is in reality a fairly unprincipled struggle, particularly evident at times of institutional threat but present all the time nevertheless.

It follows that the demand for academic freedom, when made by academics, is normally a high-flown way of pressing the (possibly quite justified) rights of their own disciplinary grouping. It can hardly be justifiable for those who ordinarily do not identify with the academic community at large to rely on that very notion when their own activities are threatened.

The argument should not be mistaken. It is not being suggested that claims to academic freedom are unjustified. Quite the reverse. It is that academics do not customarily entertain a sufficiently large enough view of academic freedom. Because their professional identity lies with their own discipline, there is a general failure to notice those larger threats to academic freedom which affect the academic community as a whole.

The point, though, needs to be pressed further. For the fragmentation of the academic class into disciplinary sub-cultures (Becher, 1981) is accompanied by the narrowing of vision that typifies small societies. Being relatively small and insular (despite being global invisible colleges), they come to form their own culture. It is a culture of language, concepts, form of interaction and underlying tacit presuppositions (about what counts as an acceptable theory and so on). It is one's mastery of the culture, so that it becomes less an alien culture than a taken-for-granted form of life that characterizes one's identity as a full member of the group. For any academic, academic freedom is none other than the freedom to live a particular form of life, to play particular language games, to interact with this rather than that set of other academics.

If this were all, things would not be so bad. But there is a more negative corollary. The narrowness of the small community has several deleterious consequences. First, as indicated, the disciplinary community sustains its own identity around a limited number of ways of going on – paradigms, theories, concepts, tacit presuppositions. The upshot is that it is difficult, though admittedly not impossible, for alternative ways of going on to get a hearing. It is clear enough why this should be so: alternative concepts and theories would constitute a rival paradigm; they would represent a threat to the way in which the disciplinary community defines and understands itself. More than that, they would constitute an attack on the personal academic identities of those who have, over many years, established their own status and credentials by faithfully working within the paradigm (Bernstein 1971, p. 56).

Attempts, therefore, to offer a new perspective do more than rock the boat. They are hardly less than mutiny, and must be treated accordingly. In fact, through control over journal publications and influence over book publications, it is possible substantially to hinder the new paradigms from ever getting an effective hearing, and so slow, if not stop, the snowballing effect of what might be an intellectual revolution.

The moral of these observations is clear enough: constraints on academic freedom are imposed just as much by the academic community itself as from outside. It should be recognized, though, that there are two forms of constraint at work within the academic community. There is the resistance met by any would-be revolutionary. And there is the self-imposed constraint on the group's 'legitimate' members.

This self-imposed constraint is a voluntary submission by the members to confine their intellectual efforts within certain parameters. There lies security, safety, conviviality, familiarity. It is accompanied by a disinclination to try something completely different, to garner resources from other intellectual fields, to venture into unfamiliar territory. Certainly that happens, but what is at issue here is the dominant current of intellectual work. It is, to employ Gellner's imagery, a rubber cage (Gellner 1980); but it is a cage less imposed upon the academic community than it is imposed by the sub-communities upon themselves.

Autonomy, neutrality and disinterestedness

It might be thought that these somewhat abstract remarks have little to do with issues of academic freedom. For reflections on the sociology and epistemology of academic knowledge seem to be tangential to matters of individual rights and freedoms. There is little here to suggest that fundamental rights of academics as academics are being threatened, particularly since (on the argument here) the academics are themselves implicated in the social and institutional movements described. If there is an issue of concern to the academic community here, perhaps it is less one of the freedoms of the individual academic than it is a matter of the autonomy of institutions of higher education? (Kleinig 1982). For surely, again on the argument here, what is of most concern is the way in which higher education has been incorporated into the modern state, thereby surrendering the historical autonomy of the separate institutions.

That indeed is an acceptable reading of the situation, but it is only part of the story. Clearly, there are issues of institutional autonomy, and these are likely to become ever more evident as, for example, contracts (Department of Education and Science (DES) 1987a) and 'improved' methods of financial accountability (DES 1987b) are established. And it makes sense to distinguish these issues from those arising from threats to the rights of members of the academic community to sustain their professional rights and responsibilities. The diminution of opportunities to secure tenure is one of these latter issues, though how far that actually does constitute a threat to academic freedom is a moot point (Tight 1985).

Nonetheless, having clearly labelled issues as warranting either the academic freedom *or* the institutional autonomy label, there is more to be said. The key point is simply that, as the foregoing argument has implied, issues of both academic freedom and institutional autonomy – where they surface today – are joint reflections of the incorporation of academe into society. The general situation is not a matter of debate; it is accepted as a *fait accompli*. It is well enough understood that efforts seriously to stand outside – as represented by the University of Buckingham – can happen only on a very limited scale. The complaints and the fears in relation to academic freedom and institutional autonomy are limited to skirmishes on the margin of the state–higher education relationship.

It certainly makes sense to ask if higher education can reach a *modus vivendi* with the state (Taylor 1975, p. 140). But the answer is, in one sense, quite straightforward. The evidence of the last thirty to forty years is that higher education can easily reach a *modus vivendi* with society which satisfies higher education. Actually the price being exacted presents the state with very little difficulty. For in reality it is the state which sets the price which it itself has to meet! The expectations of higher education as to the freedoms and range of autonomy that it can retain are accommodated to its perceptions of what the state will allow. Under these circumstances, higher education will find little difficulty in coming to an accommodation with the state.

In reality, of course, there is no final point of accommodation. Rather, the state of the *modus vivendi* simply shifts over time, more and more in the favour of the state. The establishment of annual budgets, rights of inspection of accounts and 'teaching' universities would have been literally inconceivable twenty years ago. But, if it is seen to be in the interests of academe, perceptions and expectations can change markedly and rapidly. And the admittedly distant spectre of the possible closure of one or more universities certainly acts as an incentive towards attitudinal change.

These internal shifts within the academic community have also affected other issues connected to the social philosophy of academic freedom. One of the justifications of the privileges accompanying academic freedom which was open to the university before its incorporation into the modern state (before the expansion of the 1960s) lay in the university's acceptance of certain restrictions. The privileges of academic freedom were tolerated by society so long as, whatever its individual members got up to, the university as a university declined to take up a particular stance on social issues. Accompanying academic freedom for its individual members, the university accepted a general policy of neutrality in the social affairs of society (Searle, *op.cit.*).

By and large, the university *is* neutral. This, though, cuts both ways. The university is able to hide behind a shield of neutrality even where there might be a consensus for it to adopt a position, though even here the university is not always able to maintain a stance of neutrality, much as it might wish to. Universities have been known to withdraw their investments from companies trading with South Africa; and it has often been the student body which has been especially influential in bringing about such a change in attitude. However, it goes against the grain: universities are not predisposed to taking up stances of that kind.

Universities are even (or perhaps particularly) reluctant to act where the activities of their own staff are concerned. Staff are, by and large, left to determine their own practices in keeping live animals and in using them for the purposes of experiments. There may be a general code of practice that a university would encourage its staff to adopt; but the university would do little to monitor its use. And the university would not itself seek to question, as a matter of principle, the use of live animals for experiments by its staff.

What this suggests is that the university may be neutral in many matters of social policy which intersect with its own affairs; but it is certainly not disinterested (cf Montefiore 1975, part 1). The university acts to preserve and further its interests both at the level of the institution and of the individual members of staff. And those interests can, in turn, be placed in a hierarchy. As an institution, the first interest of the university is its survival, by no means guaranteed today. Other interests will, therefore, be weighed in the balance.

Similarly, with the academics: they have interests which the notion of academic freedom reflects in the negative sense of 'freedom from X'. And they also have interests in the sense of 'freedom to do X'. Sometimes, one senses that amongst the 'freedoms from' that academics would like to have is the freedom from students, for students sometimes appear to academics to be depriving them of time that otherwise could be spent on a favoured research project. The freedom to teach is important; but it may well be secondary to the freedom to research in an individual academic's scale of values and interests.

Conclusions: the ethics of academic freedom

The academic community, ever since its mediaeval origins, has been intimately connected with its host society. It has been seen as important to society and worth the support of society. If that were not so, the Church and the Crown would not have competed to outbid each other with privileges granted to the mediaeval universities and to the scholars within them (Rashdall 1895, Vol. 2, Ch. XIII, 3&4). However, since the Second World War, and especially with the exponential growth in its size, higher education has been transformed from a small number of separate institutions into a large *system* of higher education. Higher education has become an institution in its own right; it is now a constitutive part of the apparatus of the modern state itself. In a post-industrial age based significantly on structures of knowledge, no modern society can afford to be without a higher education system, playing its part in society. Society has, and exerts, an interest in all that goes on within its universities and colleges. This role *within* the state is formally recognized in many European countries, where academic staff are directly seen as employees of the state. In the United Kingdom it is more disguised, but the reality is much the same. And it is this systematic relationship between higher education and the state that has resulted in the academics' right to 'academic freedom' being formalized and made explicit.

By and large, the academic community has been happy to fall in with the role cast for it. So far, a *modus vivendi* has not been difficult to strike between the academic community and the state. It is too simple to say that the explanation lies in the state confining its interest to matters of institutional accountability while leaving the academic freedom of individual members of staff untouched. For the interests of the state have certainly affected the role of the academic. Those effects have included requirements on academics to be more efficient managers of the resources provided by the state, but they have also impinged on academics' central commitments. Both the research programme and the teaching programme are heavily influenced by the overt interests of the state.

Despite this, academic freedom has not, until recently, become a key issue at the top of the agenda for the academic community. Three reasons stand out. First, the academic community, particularly in the sciences, the technologies and the proliferating areas of professional study, has undergone a cultural shift. The facts of life are seen as just that; the academic community is content to play its part in contributing to UK Inc. Secondly, the fragmentation of the academic community into discrete disciplinary sub-cultures has had precisely the effect of reducing the internal sense of community across academic fields; there is far less of a sense of being engaged on common enterprise that there was only thirty years ago. Thirdly, largely unrecognized by the academic community, its stock-in-trade – knowledge itself – has also shifted. All knowledge fields, to a marked degree, now take their bearings from society and its perceived needs, whether they be scientific, technological, professional, cultural or humanistic. The work of academics, in their role as members of the wider class of society's intellectuals, is certainly heterogeneous, but, for one reason or another, it is ideologically saturated through inevitably standing in some sort of relation to society.

In short, the interests of the academic class and of the state broadly coincide (Svennson 1987). And part of the logic of both sets of interests is a diminution in the role of the academic in modern society. There may be an academic ethic (Shils 1983), but it is an ethic concomitant with the restricted role that most members of the academic community accept for themselves. The academic is less and less a critic of society, maintaining an independent monitoring function for institutions of higher education (Brosan 1971), and more and more an underlabourer, working in a confined intellectual field, fulfilling a range of limited services for the state. The bars of the academic cage are as much self-imposed as imposed upon. It has to be an open question, therefore, whether academics in the modern world seek freedom in any serious form. It is doubtful that many would know how to use it, if it were suddenly bestowed upon them.

9

The Price of Freedom

John R. G. Turner

'Abolish academic freedom' – whatever it is

The Times recently printed excerpts from *One Thousand Things that Every Educated American Should Know*. There, along with Abraham's Bosom, Akhnaten and Alopecia, was Academic Freedom. If every educated American knows what it is, every educated Englishman does not. Mr Robert Jackson, the Under-Secretary of State for Education, who has special responsibility for higher education, has repeatedly declared that it is different for every institution, and therefore incapable of being either defined or incorporated into the Education Reform Bill. As most of the other measures in the Bill are dedicated to the abolition of academic freedom, the universities have every ground for the deepest concern. The consequences of the Bill are likely to spell disaster for the once-great universities that grew up in this once-great nation.

For Mr Jackson's position, we need look no further than the reports of the Commons Committee which sat on the Bill this February. I quote:

> Furthermore, it is necessary, within those budgets on financial and academic grounds, to achieve measures of rationalisation to strengthen the system. I make no apology for the proposition that it is *desirable* to *abolish academic freedom* to ensure that rationalisation can take place reasonably – [Interruption]
>
> [My italics, and good for the interrupter, whoever they were!]

Although Mr Jackson is unable to define academic freedom, he is quite willing to abolish it on the grounds that it stands in the way of 'rationalization', which is to say the dismissal and forcible redeployment of university staff. Elsewhere, though, he has been at pains to point out how much value the Conservative Party places on academic freedom and its defence. In a feature in *The Times* a few weeks earlier he had commended their record in passing the Education Bill of 1986, which placed a statutory obligation on universities and colleges to ensure freedom of political speech on campus, a freedom which in practice usually means the right of right-wing Tories and South African ambassadors to speak without being trampled under the rush of radical jack-boots.

Clearly, academic freedom is coming to mean all things to all politicians. Do *we* know what it means?

What academic freedom isn't

I am going to suggest that academic freedom, as distinct from various other freedoms that an academic might enjoy as a citizen or as a member of the Tottenham Hotspur Supporters Club, is merely that freedom which is necessary for the proper discharge of the academic profession. It is therefore clearly *not* the freedom which was protected under the Education Bill of 1986. *That* freedom, the right to political free speech, is not, or should not be, exclusive or proper to the academic profession any more than to any other citizen. Unless of course they be a professional politician, in which case their continued membership of a particular party or grouping will legitimately depend on just these things. *Nobody* should suffer victimization in their professional or private life on account of their political opinions; everyone should be allowed their free expression.

The only sense in which academics might need a small amount of extra protection in this respect is that they have, at least in subjects which border on issues of current public interest, no 'right to silence'. A coal miner does not *have* to say that he thinks Maggie is not too bad after all. Mr Raymond Honeyford was not obliged to publish articles criticizing the child-raising practices of the patrons of his school. But lecturers in sociology are under some obligation to speak their minds on social policy: dissembling motivated by fear would be corrupt, and expedient silence interpretable as culpable non-productivity and inactivity, especially in the coming days of the assessment of academic performance. And of course, if academics have free speech in their place of employment, it is only right that speakers whom they or their students invite should have the same freedom of expression. The statutory protection which these speakers have now been afforded (although recent events at Wolverhampton Polytechnic show that the Act is a paper tiger when it comes to enforcing the matter) gives an incidental protection to the academics themselves. So far it has been rare, to say the least, for them to need it (only the recent case at Ruskin College comes readily to mind), but perhaps in the future, as the rest of academic freedom is eroded away, we will come to be grateful for this special codification of one of our basic rights as citizens.

The freedom which the Tory Party is so proud of having defended is therefore not academic freedom at all, but a basic right of all members of a free society. At the other end of the scale, I suggest that academic freedom is not to be equated merely with matters of administrative autonomy between vice-chancellors and the government. The vice-chancellors may well be annoyed when the government dictates the level of fees for overseas students, and Lord Annan has recently twitted them for making this an issue of academic freedom. It does not seem particularly useful to spread the concept quite so widely, although if the vice-chancellors did make that plea (I have not researched the matter and must take Lord Annan's word for it), then they certainly had a case for doing so in terms of political tactics. Slow erosion is the policy of the government, and it will always plead, when taking away a freedom, that what it is doing is only very slight, and that it intends to do nothing more (cf. 'This is my last territorial claim in Europe' Adolph Hitler *passim*). In this way it will eventually take academic freedom away altogether. Insofar as the overseas fees were the tip of this wedge, the vice-chancellors were right to be alarmed, and we should note the use of the double-headed penny by the government: forcing the universities to capitulate quietly in the first stages of the attrition, or to appear ridiculous even in the eyes of some of their own members by treating a little issue of fiscal policy as a great one of true liberty!

What academic freedom is

Academic freedom is [to adapt the definition in the *Great Columbia Encyclopedia*] the right of academics, and other scholars who need to exercise the same functions, to pursue research, to teach and to publish, without control, restraint or the threat of sanctions from the institutions that employ them. To the Committee of Vice-Chancellors and Principals, it is the right of scholars to question current orthodoxy and received opinions, and to publish unorthodox or unpopular (or, I would add, downright perverse) views, without placing their livelihoods in jeopardy.

Those definitions, which appear in various places with variations in wording which I would not care to pick over, seem to me to be eminently plain and valid descriptions of the concept of academic freedom. Why then, it may be asked, do academics need this kind of freedom over and above the freedom of expression granted to every citizen, over and above free speech in public and private places?

If academic freedom is not simple freedom of speech, it *is* an extension of the principle of free speech which is an essential prerequisite for the proper performance of the profession. Academics need the freedom to criticize in ways which, were they working for a commercial employer or even directly for the state, might lead to sanctions by their employer. To put it simply, everyone has free speech within the law, but nobody expects this to extend to public criticism of employers, sponsors, patrons or customers. As the nation's industries, government, and indeed the whole of the nation are the sponsors, customers and patrons of the universities, additional freedom is required if the academic profession is to be exercised freely, openly and without corruption.

The academic profession cannot be properly exercised if the ecologists are to be told to shut up about pollution because they are jeopardizing the £250,000 grant to the engineering department from Great Chemical Industries plc. Yet in most professions, losing one's employer a quarter of a million would be considered more than sufficient grounds for the boot! Employees who blow the whistle on the criminal activities of their firms are public benefactors, but must hope that their public spirit will be rewarded with a job from *another* employer.

Academic freedom is not therefore some arcane and anachronistic privilege. It is to the academic profession what judicial independence is to judges, freedom of conscience to the clergy, the protection of sources of information to the journalist, parliamentary privilege to the MP, the exercise of clinical judgement to the doctor, the right of hot pursuit to the policeman. It is the simple and basic condition for the job.

It follows from the above definitions, that there is an important and less often recognized extension of academic freedom: perhaps we should speak, as did the recent petition to the Lords that originated in the London School of Economics, of academic *freedoms*. If we are to be free to speak, and publish and teach what we honestly, if often mistakenly, believe to be the case, or to be worth postulating, then there must go with that a considerable freedom to choose what subject we will investigate. To restrict the field of investigation is to restrict the nature of the results that can be obtained. It *was* a denial of academic freedom when unbearable private pressure was brought on researchers in the longitudinal study of the XYY chromosome condition in man to abandon the project, by people who simply did not like the idea of an answer being obtained. To tell someone not to investigate something is tantamount to telling them they cannot announce the result of an investigation.

A further academic freedom, I suggest, is for universities to make collective decisions of their own about the fields which they wish to develop and pursue. As this right is entrepreneurial, it is clearly subject to much more compromise with the other institutions of our society than are the other freedoms. Similarly, the other freedoms are not absolute. The freedom of publication is restricted by the law relating to official secrecy, libel, sedition, obscenity and copyright, and the freedom of investigation by legitimate public concerns for safety and the ethical use of experimental subjects (both human and animal). Debates about these aspects, though, are debates about safety, ethics and obscenity etc., not about academic freedom *per se*.

Who lacks academic freedom?

Academic freedom is not possessed by all scientists or scholars, not by a long way. Military and industrial scientists clearly do not and cannot have it, although the research directors of our better great industries do believe in releasing as much of their commissioned research material as is commercially prudent. Less obviously and less familiarly, it is not possessed, at least on paper, by the scientific civil service. Clearly, their research topics are dictated by the policy needs of the nation (which is not to say that scientific civil servants cannot propose and if approved pursue research of their own devising), but less obviously publication is always subject to clearance from their superiors, with the usual can-carrying protocol right up, in the last resort, to ministerial level. It is quite surprising to find in what non-secure areas scientific civil servants may have been required to sign the Official Secrets Act, and it has happened that this fact has been used to stop the more independently-minded from rocking the boat.

Surely, one thinks, researchers in the humanities are never similarly fettered. I know myself of only one instance where they are: the authors of official histories do not have the right to publish their findings as they see fit. The commissioning department, be it the War Office or whatever, has the final right of veto, quite over and above anything that might come under the heading of an official secret.

The threat to academic freedom

If it is true that the price of liberty is eternal vigilance, it is also true that all freedoms must be monitored lest they be abused. If academia had been turning itself into a separate estate of the realm, threatening the freedoms of other citizens, spreading sedition and attempting to set up a one-party state, then society would have a grievance. I have neither seen nor heard any suggestion that there have been abuses of this kind. The one abuse that there has been is the protection of the inefficient, the ineffective and those who have decided to take early retirement while still drawing their salaries. It is impossible to say how many academics have fitted into this category. Everyone can point a finger at someone down the corridor, but one never knows how much this is due to plain malice. We all think that we work so much harder than everyone else; 'those other idlers' are just infuriating! I believe real cases are rare: I personally have never worked alongside one. Nevertheless, the apparent absence of effective sanctions against such academics is now costing the universities dear: the Secretary of State for Education sees it as an excellent pretext for abolishing academic freedom altogether.

I do not propose to go into a clause by clause analysis of the Education Reform Bill: at the time of writing the Secretary of State, after considerable lobbying, has offered unspecified amendments, which may render obsolete any detailed exegesis. But the Bill's original consequences are worth outlining.

All the academic freedoms I have described are, or were, to be removed by the Bill, and by associated changes in the funding procedures. The Bill sought to set up machinery by which our own government could prohibit research it did not like, ban the publication of displeasing results and have dismissed from post those academics who would not comply. This was to be achieved by the combination of the abolition of tenure, the powers of direct intervention taken by the Secretary of State which would allow him to order the closure of a department, section, subsection or anything else (whereon the untenured staff would, by a strict and reasonable interpretation of the employment legislation, be redundant), and the otherwise unnoticed fact that under the new 'contracting' arrangements the government would own the copyright of all academic work and therefore would control its publication. The detailed powers of the Secretary of State, by which he could order the new Universities Funding

Council (UFC) to make very explicit instructions to particular institutions (even down to directives concerning individual members of staff, or broad classes of staff such as those espousing certain opinions), and to fine those which did not comply, have been widely discussed in *The Times* and *The Times Higher Education Supplement* during January and February 1988. The only dissension in the academic community seemed to be over the government's motives. Those adhering to the conspiracy theory of history saw a heinous plot to commence the stifling of free speech in general, during the process of setting up a Bonapartist state. Adherents of the cock-up theory saw only that academic freedom stood in the way of Mr Jackson's 'reasonable rationalizations', and was therefore to be removed purely as a matter of expediency.

Whatever the truth of that, despite all the assurances about 'strengthening academic freedom' made in the press, in answer to a planted parliamentary question and in letters to individual academics from the Under-Secretary, measures were introduced in Parliament to eliminate it. The abolition of tenure would mean that, subject only to protracted and expensive law-suits taken *after* dismissal, academics could be dismissed for 'inefficiency' or 'incompetence', which could include holding 'wrong' opinions, or for 'redundancy', which could include being in a department the government wanted to shut, or for 'financial exigency,' which could include being at the top of the pay scale! The new funding arrangements via the UFC are likely to mean that *no* research can take place that does not have higher approval from Whitehall, a Research Council or a sponsoring industry. The Secretary of State for Education also tried to take powers to direct the internal affairs of universities. He could for instance, have ordered the closure of a department, along with the consequent dismissal on grounds of 'redundancy' of all the members of staff, or prohibited or demanded the appointment of staff with any chosen shade of opinion. We could have seen, we might yet see, individuals and departments whose findings were displeasing to government or to sponsoring industries told to shut up or be shut down.

The abolition of the right to free publication exists potentially, but at the time of writing it is neither clear when and how it will be used, nor what opposition is likely to be mounted to it. The Department of Health and Social Security already claims 'intellectual property' rights over the research which it commissions, in such a way that it could, if it so desired, demand the suppression of results and conclusions which did not please Whitehall.

We do not of course use Stalinist methods in this country: I doubt if a really direct threat would be made by any administration of the type we have enjoyed so far. But the real fear that departments producing displeasing conclusions would be high on the hit-list at the next round of 'reasonable rationalization' would be quite enough to commence the slow stifling of independent expression, and start the universities on the road to being the pathetic toys of the state that one sees in certain other countries. Even our own present government has shown itself to be very vigorous in restricting the dissemination of information which it believes would be better kept from the general population. There is no need to think of anything as dramatic as the *Spycatcher* affair: the public can gain no access to orders made on industries in the realm of environmental safety. It is clear that the provisions of the current legislation would slowly be used in line with these other devices to restrict the flow of information, to muffle, quietly and slowly, the free dissemination of thought, opinion and information that still comes out of the universities.

If these last comments of mine seem 'over the top', I must simply draw attention again to a statement by Mr Jackson in Committee:

> In most continental countries dons are civil servants employed by the state. Some of the greatest universities in the history of mankind were created on that basis. The university of Berlin was a limb and branch of the Prussian state.

The Secretary of State for Education has said repeatedly that the powers he intended to take in the Bill were reserve powers only, which he never (well, hardly ever) intended to use. As it was repeatedly pointed out to him that his successors might not be so scrupulous (what for instance would happen when a latter-day Keith Joseph found some more 'Marxists' at the Open University, or a Ken Livingstone discovered a 'racist' in an anthropology department?) we seem to be left with only one question: is the man a fool or a liar?

In summary, whatever the outcome of the debates on the Education Reform Bill, which will be known to my readers but are not known to me at the time of writing, the universities should take great heed of the lesson they have been taught: academic freedom is not something this Government likes to countenance. If it failed to abolish it this time, we can be sure that that is not the last we have heard of the matter.

Lastly, the very strong links which universities are now developing with industry could pose a less direct threat to academic freedom. That paying the piper clearly means calling the tune for the commissioned work is not necessarily a problem: that is the legitimate price of industrial collaboration. The corruption starts when industry starts to lean on other operations within the university which it sees as a threat: 'Shut up about pollution, or we'll withdraw the chemical engineering grants.'

Who are its enemies?

Everyone, of course. Among the enemies of academic freedom we would have to list academics. This is particularly true of certain senior academics who would like everyone to agree with them, and who would be the direct beneficiaries of Mr Baker's Bill. Once there is a possibility of booting people out of the university on one pretext or another, it cannot but be the case that those powerful academics – who must now restrict the use of their powers to blocking the appointment of their enemies and intellectual opponents to chairs and other senior positions, and discretely scuppering their publications and grant applications when they get the chance (I have a treasured letter from a senior colleague telling me 'If you persist in publishing this viciously misleading rubbish, you can take the consequences') – would extend their operations to levering people out of a job. When it comes to the removal of the 'incompetent', we should all remember how high is the correlation between 'don't know what they're talking about' and 'fundamentally disagrees with my point of view'. One of the only sensible things that Secretary of State Baker has said during the present proceedings is that academics need protection from other academics more [well, as much at any rate] than they do from politicians.

Among other enemies of academic freedom we must number, needless to say in view of their present record, the government; also the Left and the National Union of Students, who undermine it by wanting to see freedom of political speech restricted to speakers whose opinions they approve of; the Right (of course); and, sadly, the Association of University Teachers, who in the debacle at Southampton attempted to remove freedom of academic speech (in the form of speaking at an international congress to which they had been invited) from a group of speakers purely on the ground of their national origin. They were, of course, South Africans, and if you are saying 'quite right too' then please number yourself among the enemies of academic freedom!

Lastly, there is the public. The image of the freely investigating academic is of the obsessional monomaniac pursuing trivia of no possible interest to anyone but a fellow maniac, or idle duffers indulging their hobbies. The government's attempts at abolition will receive little opposition from outside academia.

What use is academic freedom?

Can something which so many people want to see abolished be justified? I suggest that academic freedom stands as one of the freedoms which a free society should value, cherish and maintain. A society which erodes or abolishes it is destroying a part of its civilized values, and may go on to destroy the others. It has been wisely said that the first target of those who wish to set up dictatorships is freedom of speech, the freedom of academics included. It is unfortunately becoming believable that that is the course our country is setting itself on. Whether or not the present government contains members who wish to sail in that direction, it is assuredly the case that once freedoms of this kind are abolished, the way will be that much easier for the totalitarians to come in after them and finish the job.

There is also one rather clear utilitarian argument in favour of the freedom of investigation. It is that one of the best aids to true invention is not knowing what cannot be done. Radar was developed during the Second World War, we are told, by building up the team entirely from fully qualified *biologists*. Totally unaware of the impossible, they went ahead and created it. I recently encountered the graduate student of a well-known inventor who (the inventor) had developed a widely used and highly profitable industrial technique in total ignorance of the fact that no fewer than eighteen papers had previously been published showing that it was impossible. An application to a research council could only have met with rejection on the standard ground that the man had not done his homework. The passing of all scientific academic research through monitoring committees and refereeing panels, who are always only too willing to spot the missing references, point out that they (the referees) have already demonstrated that this idea is *quite wrong*, and generally dictate what subjects are open to investigation, closed to investigation, or plain out of fashion, can only stifle much valuable invention.

Finally, I would say that now is not the time in history to put independent scientific enquiry into a bureacratic strait-jacket, with a strong eye on industrial and commercial profit. Our determination, as a species, to extract these maximum profits, allied to our hyper-exponential population growth, are putting our species on a course which it is increasingly difficult to distinguish from a desperate sprint up the down escalator. We are destroying the rainforests of the tropics at the rate of 100 acres a minute, and exterminating 50 species a day in the process. Nobody knows what effects that will have: it is unlikely that the effects will be small and impossible that they should be beneficial. We are all engaged in one way or another in this destruction of the renewable resources of our planet and its capital stock of non-renewable resources. We have an economic system which is predicated on the assumption that today's investors can be paid off tomorrow by consuming some hitherto untouched or unowned resource, either of fossilized energy or mineral stock, or of wild land that can be opened for agriculture: in a finite world, that just cannot go on for ever! We desperately need solutions. To repeat: this is no time to set up a system which will permit only those scientific investigations which are so bland that they cause offence to nobody. We need people with all the originality and bloody-minded independence we can find.

The issues of expediency

The points on which the government stuck firm in February 1988 were the crucial ones. The Secretary of State could forgo all the powers of intervention he liked, and academic freedom could still be destroyed by two simple measures both taken, at least ostensibly, on the grounds of fiscal expediency: the abolition of tenure and the restructuring of the funding system. The trouble is that freedom, like everything else that is worth having (even solar energy), has its cost. If academics have tenure, they cannot be easily dismissed or redeployed when someone thinks it would be nice to save their salaries. The government in 1988 was reeling from what it had cost them in special compensation payments to decimate (literally, in the classical sense) the staff of British universities a couple of years before. Their next decimation clearly had to be cheaper, with the possibility of opening and shutting parts of academia without the kind of effective resistance they had encountered the first time round. So tenure had to go, and if academic freedom went with it, too bad. The problem that then arose was that the Secretary of State saw any attempt to introduce statutory protection of academic freedom into the Bill as a covert way of sneaking tenure back in, and nobody on the university side seemed able to think of any *effective* way of protecting academic freedom other than by some form of tenure. The result is a deadlock, and a sore of mistrust between government and universities which may take years to heal over.

Further, once academic research becomes expensive, there must be a public interest in seeing that the money is well spent. The freedom to investigate cannot include the freedom to spend unlimited amounts of other people's money in the process. This is the final dilemma: much scientific research is no longer free in the true sense, because it requires extra funding in the form of grants, and these are subject to all the stifling and corrupting effects of the vetting and refereeing system that I have described. Up to now, a small mitigation of this effect, for inexpensive research only, has existed through the University Grants Committee's (UGC) dual funding system: small amounts of money are available to all academics via the general funds of their university to pursue research entirely of their own choosing. On top of that, quite considerable funds are paid to them to be free investigators, in the form of a proportion of their own salaries, currently reckoned for UGC accounting purposes at 40 per cent.

In the name of public accountability for public money, this small zone of free operation is also about to be removed. The research element in the UGC budget will in all probability be passed not to the new UFC, but to the research councils, who will develop procedures for controlling the way it is spent. It is virtually certain that the high cost of the salary element has not escaped the government's notice, and that this too will shortly come under some form of central state control. The loss of academic freedom will be complete.

Academic freedom is not free. My estimate is that the research of the average academic scientist, in terms of their salary, the salaries of ancillary staff and the general research funding, now runs at around £11,000 per year (after allowing that tax and national insurance are regained by the state). The question seems to be 'How much will the country pay for the maintenance of a basic liberty?' At a time when the country is willing to countenance the dismantling of the welfare state and the National Health Service, I cannot be optimistic about the answer.

Note

The Education Reform Bill was finally passed by the Commons on 19 July 1988. The Jenkins–Seear amendment, originally inserted by the Lords against the Government's wishes, which gave statutory protection to individual academic freedom, was allowed to stand; but the Swann amendment, designed to mitigate direct Government control over academic matters, was fatally altered.

10

So What is Academic Freedom?

Malcolm Tight

Introduction

What conclusions can be drawn about academic freedom from the contributions to this book, and from the various arguments and analyses published in the
literature? I cannot resist starting by quoting the conclusion presented in
another edited volume on much the same subject, published in the United
States in 1983:

> As the contributors to this collection make clear, there is little consensus
> regarding the meaning of academic freedom although there is agreement
> that it is something worth protecting. The concept has been invoked in
> support of many contrary causes and positions. It, for example, was used
> to justify student activism and to repress it, to defend radical faculty and to
> defend their suppression, to support inquiry into admissions or promotion
> or tenure decisions and to deny such inquiry. It is, at best, a slippery
> notion, but clearly a notion worthy of analysis.
>
> (Kaplan and Schrecker 1983, p. 6)

At first glance it might seem reasonable to draw much the same conclusions
from the present volume, but this would not be a wholly valid assessment. For in
at least one of the contributions to this book, that by Barnett, there is a clear
implication that academic freedom is *not* something worth protecting; or rather,
to be strictly accurate, that the behaviour of British academics would seem to
indicate that many of them hold this view. And there is supporting evidence for
this interpretation in some of the other chapters. Neave emphasizes the
swiftness of the changeover in British higher education from self-regulation
within a facilitatory state to what he terms 'conditional autonomy', something
which would surely not have been achieved without some degree of acquiesc-
ence on the part of academics. In the contributions by O'Hear and Turner, on
the other hand, one can detect a sense of betrayal (see also Griffith 1987).

Yet most of the remainder of the quotation holds good, even if the examples
given necessarily have an American flavour about them. There is much in the

preceding chapters to confirm that there is little consensus, in a primarily British context, regarding the meaning of academic freedom, where it is also regularly invoked in support of many contrary causes and positions. The notion is as slippery as ever, but the present group of authors obviously retain a belief that it is worthy of analysis. One can only presume, since you have troubled to read this far, that you share some of this interest.

So let us probe a little further in this final chapter, and in doing so try to pull together the main threads of the discussion so far. I propose to do this by examining a series of basic questions, which seem to me to run through most of the contributions. I will not attempt to answer them definitively, but will try instead to suggest frameworks within which they may be considered. Inevitably, there is some degree of overlap between the ten questions identified. They are, in order of discussion: (1) What are the values which underlie academic freedom? (2) What is academic freedom for? (3) Who gets academic freedom? (4) What is the position of students? (5) What is the relationship between academic freedom and institutional autonomy? (6) What is the relationship between academic freedom and general human rights? (7) What is the relationship between academic freedom and tenure? (8) What are the implications of all this for academic structures and practices? (9) What responsibilities does academic freedom confer? and, finally, (10) What is academic freedom?

1 What are the values which underlie academic freedom?

Obviously, any individual's interpretation of academic freedom will depend upon that individual's values, modified no doubt by circumstances. This is evident in all the contributions to this volume, and is made very explicit in some of them. Goodlad, for example, states that his moral position has its roots in 'Christian tradition, filtered through Enlightenment rationalism and existentialist criticism of rationalism'. Interestingly, this would seem to parallel, at least in outline, the historical development of western universities, and it also hints at some of the ever-present tensions and conflicts between succeeding and competing values.

For, though we may trace the origins of academic freedom to the need of the early universities to protect themselves and their members from religious or political dogmatism and persecution, these same universities, through their practices and patronage, themselves gave support to particular religious, political and educational values, while opposing others (see, for example, Fuchs 1964; Minogue 1973; Paulsen 1906). Indeed, as O'Hear makes clear, institutions carrying the label 'university' may adopt widely differing values even at the same time and within the same country.

Developing these ideas a little further, it is possible to identify, at least for the purposes of discussion, four main interlocking value systems that underpin academic freedom. These operate at different levels, and will be referred to as personal, professional, institutional and societal (cf the classification used in

Becher and Kogan 1980, and referred to in Goodlad's chapter). The alternative approaches and interpretations which are employed by those concerned with higher education, operating both within and between these different levels, simultaneously condition the operation of academic freedom and create many of the problems which it is intended to avoid.

The personal level

The first level, with which this section began, is concerned with the standards of behaviour and ethics we adopt and develop for ourselves (Passmore 1984). The focus here is both individual and outward-looking. It concerns the use which we make of academic freedom, both personally and in consort with others, in pursuing understanding and truth, in investigating subjects of interest, in creatively seeking possible solutions to problems, and in communicating our findings to others. And it also concerns the ways in which we choose to relate to other academics, hopefully seeking to encourage rather than restrict their exercise of their academic freedom.

The professional level

At the second level, that of professional values, there is at present a general and often unspoken acceptance – at least within western societies – of the value of democratic or semi-democratic methods of working; embodying the notion that, at least in theory, each individual is as worthy of attention and opportunity as any other. Yet, within our higher education system, this acceptance of the virtues of democracy is shackled to the master-apprentice model, which is used most obviously in determining the treatment of students but has its staff parallel in the curious closed shop arrangement known as the peer group. Through the peer group, academics defer, or at least make some pretence at deferring, to the judgements of those who have been longer in post or have been promoted over them. In doing so, they frequently also accept more general restrictions upon their methods and areas of endeavour.

The institutional level

At the third level, the institutional value system, the concept of the university remains supreme. This long surviving and much mutated institutional form might (or might not) be extended nowadays to cover polytechnics and other institutes of higher education lacking royal charters of their own. It is primarily within the institution that personal and professional value systems are expected to come together and be exercised.

The societal level

Finally, to make the whole thing work, there are the general societal or state values which constrain and cushion the operation of higher education. Put in its simplest terms, the value system working here involves an acceptance that a particular set of practices, higher education, is good or beneficial for society; therefore it is in the interests of society to try and create the best conditions within which these practices may survive and flourish.

Society's values appear to have changed considerably in recent years. We have moved some distance away from an acceptance of higher education as being good for its own sake, albeit for only a small minority of the population, and with an emphasis on individual and long-term benefits. A more pragmatic view is now taken, which seeks a fairly immediate, direct and applicable pay-off from any given investment in provision, whether teaching or research. Or, to put it another way, society's assessment of higher education – both of different kinds of higher education and of higher education as compared with other activities competing for attention or investment – in terms of its principal outputs, which might be summarized as skills, selection and socialization, has altered. Much more emphasis is now placed on saleable skills, and correspondingly less on selection and socialization, with greater productivity expected in every case (see Tight 1987).

Each of these four value systems embodies both 'freedoms from' and 'freedoms to'; conflict as well as consensus. The systems are, of course, dynamic, so the nature of academic freedom accorded or experienced will vary from time to time depending on the specific circumstances under consideration: personal characteristics, professional judgements, institutional contexts and the degree of social acceptance and support.

2 What is academic freedom for?

Academic freedom could be, and has been, claimed for any or all of the activities which academics engage in *as* academics: i.e. teaching, scholarship, research, publication, administration and learning. Traditionally, *Lehrfreiheit* applied to teaching and scholarship, with *Lernfreiheit* covering learning. The other three elements mentioned are more recent developments or extensions of the work of academics. The treatments contained in this book place rather different emphases on these elements, stressing some and not others, although all of them are referred to. Most published discussions of the concept of academic freedom tend to deal with it as seen from the perspective of the lecturer or professor, and not from that of the student or society as a whole.

The question posed by this section may seem to be fairly unproblematic:

> For, in a democratic society such as ours, it could be argued that everyone has the freedom to learn, teach, research and publish; subject only to their intellectual resources, their ability to persuade others to pay attention to

them, their possession of the limited funds required to meet publication costs, and to them not infringing the laws relating to libel, discrimination, official secrets, conspiracy, incitement to riot and so forth (which in some cases, admittedly, might impose considerable restrictions). Indeed, one could go further and argue that, providing they are prepared to accept the possible consequences of infringing the law, everybody is free to exercise academic freedom in even the most totalitarian societies.

(Tight 1985, p. 14)

Nevertheless, even in a democratic society which, in theory at least, supports academic freedom, problems rapidly arise. There are at least three main reasons for this. First, there is the question of whether academic freedom should apply only to the acknowledged specialist interests of academics, or whether it should instead be extended indefinitely to cover any teaching, scholarship, research or publication which any academic chooses to engage in. Second, there is the point already made in the previous section: academic freedom is typically exercised within academic institutions, where hundreds or thousands of individuals come together, with the inevitable potential for disagreement which that creates. And, third, there is the sobering fact that relatively little of this activity is directly and individually self-supporting. It has to be heavily underwritten by the state and other charitable or commercial interests. Hence there is plenty of scope for differences of opinion between paymasters and participants, as well as with any intermediaries who may be involved long the way.

The first of these problems seems, on the face of it, to be the most straightforward, but it attracts a great deal of attention when arguments between academics over some issue of current concern are publicized in the media (ranging from the obvious exchanges of political views to, for example, debates about the genuineness of fossils). There seems to be no reason why an academic should have any more right to exercise academic freedom in an area outside their acknowledged expertise than, say, a student or, for that matter, a member of the general public. This is not to say that academics, or anyone else, should be prevented from expressing their non-specialist views, but it should be clear that these are made in a non-academic capacity (and ideally, perhaps, should be made privately or off-campus). The difficulty, of course, lies in the word 'acknowledged' and in the existence of grades of expertise. It is, unfortunately, only too easy for those supposedly expert in a particular field to dismiss the opinions of others on the grounds that they are not themselves expert.

The institutional context creates further complications. In his chapter (see, in particular, Figure 5.1 and the related discussion), Goodlad gives a number of examples of the conflicts which can arise between academics, their institutions and their funders regarding the exercise or control of academic freedom. To some extent, such conflicts are system-specific. In the traditional *Lehrfreiheit/Lernfreiheit* schema, for example, any student who found the teaching methods or curriculum of a particular professor unsatisfactory was at liberty to go elsewhere. Despite the steady growth of credit transfer arrangements, this remedy would scarcely be a practical option in the modern British system.

Yet we have to accept that academic life is not about agreement. Whether you express its underlying aim as being the search for truth or the development and sharing of individual understanding (cf. Hawkesworth), the processes involved are intrinsically concerned with conflict. Criticism, disagreement, rebuttal and refutation are the stuff of academic work. The real issue, then, is how academics are regulated, or how they choose to regulate themselves, so as to minimize the disadvantageous consequences of conflict while nurturing its positive aspects.

This is where administration becomes of great importance and where, in many cases, the lie is given to the ideal of democratic working. And administration is naturally of special significance when it is linked to financial dependency. Although the financial controls exerted over academic teaching are increasing, through the gradual extension and growing comprehensiveness of contractual arrangements, these have had relatively little impact as yet upon course content and teaching methods. They have, however, effectively denied an undetermined number of potential students the chance of a higher education, and prevented the recruitment of additional staff. But it is in the area of research – as distinct from scholarship, which tends to be more personal and thus cheaper – that the difficulties for academic freedom caused by the need for financial support are probably most apparent.

Research in institutions of higher education has, of course, been substantially funded by government for many years, either directly through research councils and other agencies, or through the block grant support given to institutions to establish 'well-found' laboratories, libraries, computing networks and other facilities. In recent years there has been, as Barnett notes in his chapter, an increased differentiation between pure or basic research and strategic or applied research, with a steady shift in financial support towards the latter. This trend has affected research students, with the expansion of the various linked studentship schemes, as well as research undertaken by academics as individuals or in groups. It could even be said to have extended into undergraduate teaching through the use of sandwich placements and practical projects.

The sponsors of research, whether they are a central government department, another public authority or a private firm, may have very different (and perhaps no less worthy) motivations, priorities and expectations from those of the academic researcher. This can affect not just the structure and methodology of the research, but also the way in which any findings are interpreted, and whether and how they are subsequently published or disseminated. There are numerous cases in both the sciences and the social sciences where the researchers concerned feel that their sponsors have interfered unduly, and sometimes to their personal detriment, in the conduct of research (see, for example, Caudrey 1987, Wenger 1987), and these are not confined to sensitive areas of government policy and industrial practice. Such conflicts might have been avoided if the terms on which the research was undertaken had been more clearly negotiated and understood by all the parties concerned before the work was begun, and if such agreements had then been strictly adhered to. Clearer contracts woud not, however, get around the difficulties of not being able accurately to anticipate the results of research well in advance of its completion.

There are two important qualifying points here. First, it seems reasonable that the party funding a piece of academic research – or any other piece of academic work – should have some say in how that work is pursued. She who pays the piper should be able to, if not exactly call the tune, at least indicate her general musical tastes and intervene in some way if the notes become too discordant. Second, and more fundamentally, acceptance of the principle of academic freedom does not and cannot imply that funding will somehow be provided for each and every venture that an academic wishes to engage in.

3 Who gets academic freedom?

If we agree that academic freedom is for teaching, scholarship, research, publication, administration and learning, then it seems logical that those who get academic freedom should be teachers, scholars, researchers, publishers, administrators and learners. But a number of conditions need to be attached to this statement. First, academic freedom is here being taken to apply to individual academics raher than to their employing institutions. Second, academic freedom only applies to *academics* engaged in teaching, scholarship, etc., and not to other groups, whether these are professional (e.g. secondary school teachers, adult trainers) or lay (e.g. amateur historians). And, third, any individual academic would not necessarily be given academic freedom for all of the activities mentioned, but only those deemed appropriate; just as, as already noted, they would not normally be given it for activities beyond the scope of their acknowledged expertise.

However, deferring the question of students to the following section, two difficulties remain, neither of which is substantially addressed in any of the other contributions to this book. These are, on the one hand, 'what is an academic?', and, on the other, 'should all academics get academic freedom?'.

The definition of an academic may seem to be a rather pedantic exercise, but a little thought serves to show that this is not the case. For the academic profession, greatly expanded during the 1960s and early 1970s, and hemmed in ever since then, is in a very strange state today. The profession has aged significantly, even though large numbers of elderly members of staff have opted, whether at the first opportunity or under considerable pressure, to take early retirement packages (though these often include an agreement to subsequently re-employ the staff member concerned on a part-time basis). Are these people academics? From the treatment of those who remain active, it would seem so.

At the other end of the profession, there are those young academics 'fortunate' enough to have been employed on short-term contracts, and who are now unlikely ever to enjoy the fruits of tenure even if they are able to continue in academic careers. And we should not forget the uncounted heads who, under different or more favourable circumstances, might have got academic posts but did not, yet still retain some academic connections and interests. Are these people academics? If we accept that the latter group are, then we are bound to conclude that the link between an academic and an institution of higher education can be very tenuous indeed. If that is the case, there seems to be no real reason why any aspiring individual should not be treated as at least an honorary academic.

However, the acceptance of an individual as an academic need not mean that the individual is granted academic freedom, at least not complete academic freedom. Some kind of hierarchy may be in operation, as, for example, in the Humboldtian system described by Neave (see also Pincoffs 1975). Full academic status and freedom might only be accorded to established professors and/or heads of department and denied to, or made probationary for, all other lecturers, researchers, assistants and administrators working in academic institutions. Something like this system operates in the United Kingdom at the present time, though in a less extreme form. Lecturers entering the profession are normally expected to satisfactorily complete a probationary period before they are given a more secure contract. Researchers on short-term contracts are effectively on continual probation. And even established academics are subject to the judgements of their peer groups when they seek research funds or wish to publish their findings. Very few, if any, academics enjoy what might be called full academic freedom, the ability to do what they wish in an academic context with no expectations imposed and no comeback possible.

There is, of course, another interpretation of the question posed, one expressed in the chapter by O'Hear. This would confine academic freedom to a particular class of academics: those working in 'universities' established on, in this case, the Newman/Leavis model. Those working in other kinds of institution (i.e. polytechnics, colleges, many present day universities), or in other ways (e.g. applied teaching and research), would neither be granted academic freedom nor be thought to need it. In this context it is interesting to note that 'academic drift' within the British higher education system now seems to be flowing both ways. Not only have (some) polytechnics aspired to become more like universities in terms of their subject profile, recruitment and autonomy, but (some) universities have also become more like polytechnics by developing local industrial links. In these circumstances, it becomes increasingly difficult to tell institutions apart (Tight 1988), and relatively few academics would qualify, in O'Hear's terms, for academic freedom of any sort.

4 What is the position of students?

It is not sufficient to rely solely on the historical notion of *Lernfreiheit* in considering what elements of academic freedom students may have a need for or an entitlement to. Times have changed. Students are not infrequently involved nowadays in rather more than simply learning (e.g. in small-scale research), and others than students are also involved as learners (e.g. staff).

Following the general tone of the preceding two sections, it may be argued that students should be accorded the academic freedoms relevant to their needs. Such an interpretation would not, in most cases, give students any academic freedoms beyond those of learning, plus a certain amount of scholarship and research, in their particular fields of interest. They would not, for example, any more than the general public, have an automatic right to a say in the control of teaching or research, or in the management of the institutions which they attend or receive instruction from. Nevertheless, it may well be in the interests of those institutions and their staff to involve student representatives (and, for that matter, the general public) in these ways to some extent. Indeed, this is the present position in most British institutions of higher education, though, as Barnett points out, it is one which appears to be endorsed without any serious questioning by the silent majority of the student population.

The odd and distinctive mood of the 1960s, when students rebelled against the disciplines imposed by their institutions, seeing them as reflecting the outdated attitudes of a restrictive society and a guilty older generation (see, for example, Caine 1969, Hook 1970, Searle 1972), has been replaced by one which is far more pragmatic and instrumental. It would seem that many present-day students do not want academic freedom, or, as Barnett concludes with regard to staff, would not know what to do with it if they were suddenly given it. But perhaps it would be in their best interests if they were, for higher education is hardly about spoon-feeding. Students should surely, as Goodlad argues, be encouraged to participate in determining what they study and how they go about it, to engage in a process of personal and group exploration. And, if they cannot or will not accept such a share in the responsibility for learning, then perhaps they are not really mature or able enough to – in the words of the reformulation of the Robbins' principle drafted by the University Grants Committee and the National Advisory Body – 'benefit from higher education' (NAB 1984; UGC 1984).

On these grounds entry to higher education might be granted much more readily than it is at present to mature students, who, on the basis of their experience as much as their formal qualifications, can demonstrate that they are able to make a significant contribution to teaching and learning processes. The acceptance of such a view would, of course, imply substantial changes in current institutional practices. But any opening up of access to higher education in this way could not – any more than in the case of other elements of academic freedom – be taken to embody an outright entitlement to the funding necessary for individuals to pursue this course of action.

5   What is the relationship between academic freedom and institutional autonomy?

Academic freedom and institutional autonomy are clearly not the same thing, though they are often discussed as if they were either synonymous or inseparable. The Robbins Report, for example, confuses the two concepts in its chapter on 'academic freedom and its scope' by first briefly considering the position of the individual teacher and then moving on to examine the main constituents of what it termed 'institutional freedom'(Committee on Higher Education 1963, chapter 16). Similar confusion is evident in many pronouncements made by other organizations and individuals, and in much of the recent discussion concerning the establishment of the Universities Funding Council (UFC). It is important, therefore, to try and disentangle the two concepts and see them in their true relationship.

That academic freedom and institutional autonomy are closely related is indicated in the various contributions to this volume, which typically discuss both concepts or even, as in Neave's chapter, focus on the latter rather than the former. But the principal distinction between the two concepts has to be the obvious one: academic freedom relates to academics, that is to individuals, whereas institutional autonomy relates to institutions, their employers. The important issue, then, is whether it is possible or desirable to have academic freedom without institutional autonomy, or vice-versa. In reviewing this issue, it is as well not to be too hidebound by existing practices and assumptions.

There is no reason to suppose, to start with, that the existence of institutional autonomy in some way guarantees academic freedom: it may be, as Rendel points out, a necessary but not a sufficient condition. After all, academic freedom is needed at least as much to protect individual academics from other academics as from politicians, priests, the press and members of the public. Academic institutions, whether autonomous or not, are quite capable of being oppressive to their individual members (or of permitting oppression by others to take place), and the great majority of cases in which academic freedom is seen as being threatened are probably of this nature. Indeed, if institutions are truly autonomous it may be much more difficult for the threatened individual to gain effective redress or appeal against their judgements.

But is academic freedom possible without institutional autonomy? The answer has to be 'yes', but with reservations. Many institutions of higher education in the United Kingdom are not autonomous in the way that our universities are usually thought of as being, although some have become more independent during the last few years as the Council for National Academic Awards (CNAA) has relaxed its controls. Much will change, of course, with the passing of the Education Reform Bill. Yet there does not appear to be much evidence that academic freedom has been significantly more threatened in polytechnics and colleges of higher education than it has been in universities (Wagner 1982). On the other hand, where institutional autonomy is virtually non-existent, as in centrally planned economies, academic freedom is less likely to exist or be maintained. It seems reasonable to conclude, therefore, that while it is possible to have academic freedom without institutional autonomy, and vice-versa, the two concepts tend to be mutually supporting and it is desirable that both should be encouraged if each is to flourish.

The apparent confusion between the two concepts appears to be due to the failure of many academics to take account of latter day changes which have overturned traditional ways of working. British universities began their history as privately owned corporations of scholars. As such they had effective institutional autonomy, and, with the support of the state and/or the church, the powers temporal and spiritual, were in a position to grant their members academic freedom. The steadily increasing reliance of the universities (and other institutions) during the twentieth century on government support, accelerating rapidly from the 1950s to the current position where the state underwrites the great majority of higher education expenditure, has effectively destroyed the traditional linkage between academic freedom and institutional autonomy. Yet, so long as the higher education system continued its remorseless expansion in the 1960s and early 1970s, the consequences of this were ignored or barely noticed by academics:

> It is plain to see that the original academic freedom of the professors to teach what they thought fit and of the students to learn as they pleased has now been debased and perverted into the claim of the universities that they shall continue as corporate bodies within the state and to a large extent supported by the state, and yet shall remain free from state control. The freedom of the individual has become lost under the blanket of freedom for the institution.
>
> (Betteridge 1969, p. 198)

The steady state or contraction which has been experienced by the higher education system since the 1970s should by now, as Barnett indicates, have made the changed nature of the relationship between government and higher education clearly apparent to all with eyes to see. Institutional autonomy, in Neave's analysis, has become conditional on higher education broadly satisfying the parameters laid down for it by government. The provisions contained in the Education Reform Bill propose to make this relationship even closer and more specific. The message is obvious. If institutions of higher education wish to increase, or even maintain, their autonomy, they will have either to demonstrate their worthiness to their present paymasters or to diversify their sources of financial support. Keith Joseph made this abundantly clear during his period as Secretary of State:

> Every step that the higher education institutions can take to increase contributions from the private sector will be a step towards the greater reality of academic freedom and real independence.
>
> (Hansard 26 October 1984, p. 912)

Some institutions had already taken note then: all are now being increasingly pushed in this direction by necessity.

6 What is the relationship between academic freedom and general human rights?

In societies where what we would regard as basic human rights – food, clothing and shelter, and then perhaps freedom of thought and expression – do not exist, the maintenance of academic freedom is likely to be difficult. Indeed, it would probably be viewed as a perverse irrelevance by most non-academics. On the other hand, as Rendel's chapter indicates, in countries which subscribe to one or more of the range of international accords which cover human rights issues, these may in essence guarantee basic academic freedoms to all those wishing to take advantage of them. The problem in such cases is whether and how these agreements are put into practice. They would be unlikely, in any event, to provide more than a general assurance that individuals were free to engage in academic pursuits without undue hindrance. The distinction being indicated here is one between 'freedoms from' and 'freedoms to'. Where general human rights are upheld, all adults may be free *from* constraints on their academic freedom, but not all are free *to* exercise academic freedom, because many lack the support or the ability to do so.

So why do we need to retain the notion of academic freedom if (and I accept that this is debatable) we already enjoy general human rights? Obviously because academic freedom confers something additional on its beneficiaries which is not already present or implied in human rights provisions. Historically, and in certain societies, this additional benefit could take the form of what Minogue has termed 'an exemption from the rigour of the law' (Minogue 1973, p. 50), but this is not the case in contemporary British society. The additional rights conferred by academic freedom nowadays could be seen as being either individually or institutionally located. Either way, if a valid division from human rights is to be maintained, academic freedom would seem to necessitate a firm commitment – albeit selective and constrained by circumstances – on the part of society to provide at least a minimal level of support in order to sustain an environment within which academic freedom might be effectively exercised.

But the relationship between these two concepts may be looked at from the other direction as well. What implications do human rights agreements have for the practice of academic freedom, and does academic freedom embody within it the values underlying human rights legislation? These questions are covered in the chapters by Rendel, Hawkesworth and Parekh. They provide evidence to suggest that academic freedom is frequently applied in ways which undermine the academic freedom of certain groups within society (e.g. women, ethnic minorities, mature students), and of those with alternative or minority views (e.g. those of Marxists). Indeed, it would seem that academic institutions are much like other institutions in this respect, reflecting their general social contexts, and that academic freedom may be readily abused by those in positions of power to permit the expression of points of view and actions detrimental to others. The implication of this is – notwithstanding that higher education is, at least partly, about the development of educational elites – that our practices require reform.

We should also review the position of the temporary or honorary academic – i.e. the person who is invited into an academic institution, or onto its campus, to give a lecture or to participate in some other way – if only because it reflects concerns dear to the heart of the present government. What standards should institutions apply in such circumstances, their own or those of society (academic freedom or civil rights), if there is a danger that these are in conflict? For it is to grossly oversimplify the situation to argue that 'freedom of speech' is guaranteed by both. Curiously, it would seem that the difficulties which have arisen with invited speakers stem more from the over-application or mis-application of academic freedom than from its disregard. Higher education institutions have, if anything, been too liberal in permitting their staff and students to bring guests, both academic and non-academic, on to the campus without due regard for their responsibilities for good order. What is regrettable is that an Act of Parliament (the Education Act (no. 2) 1986) was deemed to be necessary to force institutions to take these responsibilities more seriously; thus effectively putting universities and colleges on a par with football clubs and public houses.

7   What is the relationship between academic freedom and tenure?

The relationship between academic freedom and academic tenure is subject to at least as much misunderstanding as that between academic freedom and institutional autonomy:

> The relationship between tenure and academic freedom is symbolic, and so highly political, rather than operational.
>
> (*Times Higher Education Supplement*, 12 February 1988)

It is still widely assumed and asserted, at least at the level of public argument, that these concepts are indissolubly linked, long after the conditions which gave rise to their linkage have changed (see, for example, Moodie 1982). The practice of granting qualified academics lifelong tenure was adopted when there was a much smaller cadre of academics than there is today, and was designed to protect them from unfair dismissal in cases where their employers subsequently found their views uncongenial. This is not to say that we live today in such an enlightened age that no academics are ever again likely to be threatened with unfair dismissal, but to recognize that there are now other means available for safeguarding against this and that these methods do not suffer from the major drawbacks associated with lifelong tenure. These drawbacks are threefold: tenure has a discriminatory effect within the academic profession, it differs from practice in other professions and it is inflexible.

Tenure creates discrimination within the academic profession because it is not available to all academics. Not all universities give it to their employees, and it is uncommon in other kinds of institution; nor has tenure been given to all types of academic, even within those institutions which make us of it. Researchers, in particular, tend to be appointed on short-term contracts, even when they have been employed as such for many years, while academic administrators typically have 'standard' conditions of employment. Overall, only a minority of the British academic profession has tenure at the present time. So, if tenure is really needed for the protection of academic freedom, only a minority of academics can be considered to have academic freedom (cf. Sartorius 1975). Unless, that is, one accepts the rather fanciful arguments which would have it that the possession of tenure by some academics acts in some referred way to protect all academics.

Experience in the United Kingdom suggests that the possession or otherwise of tenure does not have much effect on individual academic freedom. The main practical distinction between tenured and contract staff seems to be that more is expected of the latter in terms of workload and productivity, while the former can, if they so choose, get away with doing much less. But this is really a management problem, not one directly concerned with academic freedom, and it would be more easily resolved if no one had tenure. Silber, however, writing in the United States in the early 1970s, argues along different lines:

> Infringement by tenured professors of the rights of nontenured faculty to develop their intellectual interests according to their own professional judgement . . . represents by far the most serious and most frequent violation of academic freedom in our colleges and universities.
>
> (Silber 1973, p. 51)

Yet even tenure is not necessarily a complete protection if your employer is really determined to get rid of you, and and it provides very little defence against more subtle forms of discrimination.

If in this country we move, as the Education Reform Bill intends, to a system where lifelong tenure is no longer given to any academic, this would put the academic profession on a par with others that have highly trained workforces (Ashby, 1973). Always excepting judges, it is difficult to think of another major profession which enjoys tenure in the same way. Certainly not school teachers, or lawyers, or priests, or accountants, or journalists, or even doctors. In such professions, experienced staff will usually have a contract which gives them security of employment but allows for their dismissal on a variety of grounds, most notably financial exigency (indeed, this is how academic tenure is interpreted in many other countries. See Chait and Ford 1982). Dismissal in these circumstances would normally involve the payment of a substantial redundancy award, with protection against unfair dismissal being provided by established procedures and the courts. Significantly, all of the professional groups mentioned have a vested interest in the pursuit of knowledge and truth and its application, as academics have, so why is it only academics that require the particular protection of lifelong tenure?

It is surely time for the academic profession to be honest with itself and recognize lifelong tenure for what it is: an unnecessary historical anachronism which is unfair in its application and grossly inflexible. Of course, few difficulties would arise if the higher education system were still expanding rapidly as it was in the 1960s, but that was always an unreal period. The tenure which was widely granted to academics then has left a bitter legacy, freezing up the system, constraining it within the structures which were then established and severely restricting the scope for any subsequent innovation (Aronowitz 1985).

Alternative and more flexible systems of tenure have been suggested at various times – e.g. restricting tenure to the professoriate, linking tenure to only a small basic salary – but these reforms have never been acted upon (Eustace 1983; Morris 1974). Tenure now needs removing rather than reforming. It could readily be replaced by normal contracts of employment, varied so as to reflect the demand for academics of different types, in different subjects and with different workloads. Ironically, the removal of tenure should improve the employment conditions of many academics, putting pressure on their institutions to grant them more competitive salaries and job packages. It should also encourage the development of more joint (e.g. with industrial companies or public authorities), part-time and specialist (e.g. teaching only) appointments.

8   What are the implications of all this for academic structures and practices?

All that has been said so far has considerable implications for academic structures and practices. These implications – for the general behaviour of academics; for their methods of teaching, assessment and research; for the organization of subject knowledge and disciplines – effect all those who enjoy the benefits of academic freedom:

> The very practice of academic freedom, through teaching, learning, research and publication, involves (or should involve) the continual assessment and criticism of the products of others' academic freedom.
>
> (Tight 1985, p. 15)

The problem then is to encourage the operation of academic freedom in ways which, while enabling constructive and worthwhile criticism to flourish, prevent or minimize abuses of these privileges with their detrimental effects for the freedoms of others.

Goodlad has indicated, in his chapter, some of the alternative good practices which can be developed in higher-level teaching and learning, such as reflection and consultation during study, problem-based study, study service. If it is accepted that students should have academic freedom, constrained as necessary by their unqualified status, then they need to be encouraged to become involved as much as possible in the organization of their learning. Since students are an increasingly heterogeneous group, this argues for a much wider variation in the higher education process in accordance with individual needs, abilities and aspirations. This requires the use of more independent, open, flexible and responsive forms of teaching and learning. Inevitably, practical problems will limit the possibilities for developments in these directions, and such developments will undoubtedly – if only because they are developments – be more demanding of, though hopefully also more rewarding to, the academics concerned. But these difficulties cannot be taken as valid reasons for disregarding the academic freedom of students.

Similar arguments apply to staff relations. The status quo of age, seniority and influence over the various institutional and disciplinary sources of power should not be used to limit the academic freedom of younger, more junior and less powerful colleagues. The operation of academic freedom requires an even-handedness of treatment which gives due consideration to the views of each and every academic – whether staff or student, teacher or researcher, male or female, employed or unemployed – even and especially if these views are at odds with currently accepted beliefs. Academics should, as Hawkesworth, Rendell and Turner argue, welcome alternative conceptions of knowledge and challenging theories, while recognizing the pitfalls of relying on claims for the objectivity of established or vested interests. Academics should not be placed in a position where they feel obliged to engage in self-censorship (a trend noted by both Barnett and Rendel), avoiding awkward or controversial subjects or methods altogether.

Academics are, of course, only human beings; although, as highly qualified and privileged members of society, high standards of behaviour might reasonably be expected of them. The maintenance of academic freedom requires that mechanisms exist for the resolution of cases where academic freedom has been threatened, or where this is claimed to have happened. Higher education is organized on a matrix rather than a line management basis, with individual academics identifying at least as much with their discipline as with the institution that employs or educates them. This suggests that two avenues for redress, based separately on institutions and disciplines, may be required in disputes concerning academic freedom, with a third set of safeguards needed to regulate dealings with the world outside academe.

At present, few institutions of higher education, disciplinary associations or funding agencies have a committee or group charged solely with the responsibility for investigating issues of academic freedom. Such issues would usually be considered, if at all, by a committee established for more general purposes. Arrangements of this sort are hardly suitable, however, since established committees will tend to reflect the very pecking orders and power bases which are involved in so many abuses of academic freedom. More open and uncommitted groups, probably composed mainly of junior staff, students and non-academics, would be more appropriate for maintaining some kind of balance. Flexibility of approach is important in this context:

> Justice in higher education is most effectively implemented if it is institutionally disaggregated instead of applied in a blanket fashion across a system.
>
> (Clark, 1983, p. 259)

Ultimately, the courts are available to those who feel that their rights have been impinged upon, but it ought to be possible for academics to regulate the great majority of their affairs without recourse to such expensive and time-consuming methods.

9 What responsibilities does academic freedom confer?

One seldom gets something for nothing in real life. Thus, while academic freedom may be given to or assumed by academics, as a privilege or as a necessary part of their job, this carries with it an inevitable *quid pro quo* in terms of expectations, responsibility and accountability. Yet this crucial aspect of academic freedom is frequently ignored; which is why, in a small attempt to redress the balance, the title *Academic Freedom and Responsibility* was chosen for this book.

Broadly speaking, there are two levels of responsibility required of academics in their exercise of academic freedom: those internal to academe and those external to it. The internal responsibilities, involving a due regard for the academic freedom of other academics, the positive encouragement of academic developments and an acceptance of the procedures adopted for safeguarding academic freedom, have been considered in the previous section. This section will, therefore, focus on external responsibilities. External accountability may be formal or informal, direct or indirect, to society in general or to its representatives (notably government, but also other bodies). It is owed to society because society is the major funder of higher education as well as its major beneficiary.

There has long been a tension between the demands for academic freedom in higher education, as variously interpreted by different people, and the demands of its funders for accountability:

> The development of mass higher education has been accompanied by what can only be termed a polarisation around these twin issues of freedom and accountability. For some, academic freedom acts as an ideology, hiding the fact that higher education is wholly at the service of the ruling groups in society or working in defence of the established social and economic order. For others, academic freedom constitutes the prime condition, the fundamental guarantee that 'the search for truth can be pursued somewhere without restraint' . . . Just as the attitudes of radicals and conservatives are apt to differ on the definition of 'academic freedom', so their attitudes on the matter of academic accountability are apt to be a mirror image of the stance taken as regards the first. To the former, accountability to a broader constituency than just the university is seen as a corrective to an autonomy which appeared to benefit only the senior ranks of university teaching staff. To the latter, the introduction of more stringent measures of accountability, in the form of direct government intervention to specify by legal fiat the distribution of power amongst the constituent elements of the university . . . was looked upon as yet a further infringement of both academic – and by extension, professorial – autonomy.
>
> Neave 1980, p. 49

The critical questions at the present time are, as Neave makes clear in his chapter in this book, how far and in how much detail should higher education be accountable to government, and should this accountability be direct or mediated through some quasi-independent body? Where, in other words, should the boundary between funder and funded be placed?

Clearly, government has in recent years shifted this boundary in its favour, so that it now requires a greater degree of accountability from higher education.

The Education Reform Bill will place even greater control in the hands of the Secretary of State. These changes will particularly effect the university sector, with the replacement of the University Grants Committee (UGC) by a Universities Funding Council (UFC), and the introduction of contract funding arrangements, whatever these may turn out to mean in practice. Most public sector institutions, as well as the Open University, have been subject to rather more stringent procedures until now.

A greater degree of specificity is already entering into funding arrangements, with an increasing proportion of the resources available being targeted nationally into favoured areas or projects. This is occurring in both teaching (e.g. science and technology provision, continuing vocational education) and research (e.g. centres of excellence, programme funding, linked studentships). The Manpower Services Commission (MSC), through the new 'Enterprise in Higher Education' programme and other schemes, is also endeavouring to exert an influence on provision, as it has done over the past decade in further education.

It is difficult to judge whether the increased accountability now being demanded of the products of academic freedom is reasonable, or whether it goes too far and itself infringes academic freedom. The impact of demands for accountability will, in any case, vary widely between individuals within higher education. But the days of 'black box' accountability, when (some) higher education institutions were given block grants and essentially left to their own devices as to how they were spent, are gone for good.

A system which embodies greater accountability may, though at times both irritating and time-consuming, turn out to be fairer and better able to prevent many abuses of academic freedom. Academics and their institutions are not merely in the business of advancing knowledge, ostensibly for the eventual benefit of society, but should also be concerned with making their discoveries and understanding available to as many as possible, explaining what they are trying to do as they do it. Accountability, if properly handled – which does not mean the insensitive application of standardized, quantified performance indicators, or the endorsement of the ill-informed opinions of a self-selected group of senior academics – can and should be positive, useful and encouraging.

10 What is academic freedom?

So what, then, is academic freedom? The Committee of Vice-Chancellors and Principals (CVCP), in their lobbying for changes in the Education Reform Bill, have recently defined it:

> . . . not as job protection for life but as the freedom within the law for academic staff to question and to test received wisdom and to put forward new and controversial or unpopular opinions without placing individuals in jeopardy of losing their jobs.
>
> (CVCP 1987b)

This definition, though apparently broadly acceptable to the Secretary of State, has not, at the time of writing, been incorporated within the Bill. Indeed, the Bill as published does not make any reference at all in its 169 pages to the concept of academic freedom. The closest it comes is in talking of 'the principles of justice and fairness' in the clauses drawn up to reform academic tenure, which enable institutions to dismiss academic staff by reason of redundancy and provide for new appeal procedures (Education Reform Bill, 1987; see also Hansard, 13 January 1988, columns 268–9).

The CVCP's definition has good features, not least its brevity, but, in the light of the arguments which have been presented in this chapter and elsewhere in this book, it lacks sufficient breadth to serve most purposes. The definition distances academic freedom from academic tenure, though it retains a job-specific context, and implies by omission a distinction between academic freedom and both institutional autonomy and human rights. But it limits the scope of academic freedom, in terms of what it is for and who it is for, and does not in itself provide either a justification for academic freedom or an indication of the returns to be expected from it.

With these points in mind, the following slightly longer definition is suggested:

> Academic freedom refers to the freedom of individual academics to study, teach, research and publish without being subject to or causing undue interference. Academic freedom is granted in the belief that it enhances the pursuit and application of worthwhile knowledge, and as such is supported by society through the funding of academics and their institutions. Academic freedom embodies an acceptance by academics of the need to encourage openness and flexibility in academic work, and of their accountability to each other and to society in general.

This definition attempts to incorporate an appreciation of the issues considered in this chapter, but at the same time deliberately leaves some scope for pluralism in interpretation. The underlying principles of academic freedom, expressed and understood along these lines, should be seen as a central tenet of academic life by all who are involved in it. They should not be treated as an empty shibboleth, to be launched into ritualized arguments when conviction and appreciation are lacking.

Bibliography

Albert, H. (1985) *Treatise on Critical Reason*. Princeton, Princeton University Press (translated by M. Rorty).

Arblaster, A. (1974) *Academic Freedom*. Harmondsworth, Penguin.

Aronowitz, S. (1985) 'Academic Freedom: a structural approach'. *Educational Theory*, 35, 1, 1–13.

Ashby, E. (1973) 'Human Right or Fringe Benefit?', *Times Higher Education Supplement*, 9 November, 13.

Ashby, E. with Anderson, M. (1966) *Universities: British, Indian, African: a study in the ecology of higher education*. Harvard University Press.

AUT Bulletin (1974) *Statement on Academic Freedom*.

Barnes, B. (1974) *Scientific Knowledge and Sociological Theory*. London, Routledge and Kegan Paul.

Barrows, H. and Tamblyn, R. (1980) *Problem-Based Learning: an approach to medical education*. New York, Springer.

Becher, T. (1981) 'Towards a Definition of Disciplinary Cultures', *Studies in Higher Education*, 6, 2, 109–22.

Becher, T. and Kogan, M. (1980) *Process and Structure in Higher Education*. London, Heinemann.

Becher, T., Embling, J. and Kogan, M. (1977) *Systems of Higher Education: the United Kingdom*. New York, ICED.

Benhabib, S. (1986) *Critique, Norm and Utopia*. New York, Columbia University Press.

Berchem, T. (1985) 'University Autonomy: illusion or reality?', *Oxford Review of Education*, 11, 3.

Bereday, G. (1973) *Universities for All*. San Francisco, Jossey-Bass.

Berger, P. and Luckmann, T. (1967) *The Social Construction of Reality*. London, Allen Lane.

Bernstein, B. (1971) 'On the Classification and Framing of Educational Knowledge', *in* M. Young (ed.) *Knowledge and Control*. London, Collier-Macmillan.

Bernstein, R. (1976) *The Restructuring of Social and Political Theory*. Philadelphia, University of Pennsylvania Press.

—— (1983) *Beyond Objectivism and Relativism*. Philadelphia, University of Pennsylvania Press.

Betteridge, H. (1969) 'Academic Freedom', *Universities Quarterly*, 23, 2, 189–202.

Bijleveld, R. (1987) *The Two Tier Structure in Dutch University Education: a first evaluation of a comprehensive innovation.* Enschede, Universiteit Twente (mimeo).

Bligh, D. (1982) 'Freedoms, Rights and Accountability', *in* D. Bligh (ed.) *Accountability or Freedom for Teachers.* Guildford, Society for Research into Higher Education.

Bloom, A. (1987) *The Closing of the American Mind.* New York, Simon and Schuster.

Bloom, B. (1956) *Taxonomy of Educational Objectives.* New York, David McKay.

Bloor, D. (1976) *Knowledge and Social Imagery.* London, Routledge and Kegan Paul.

Boud, D. (ed., 1985) *Problem-based Learning in Education for the Professions.* Sydney, Higher Education Research and Development Society.

Boudin, L. (1983) 'Academic Freedom: shall we look to the court?', *in* Kaplan C. and Schrecker, E. (eds).

Bourdieu, P. and Passeron, J. (1977) *Reproduction in Education, Society and Culture.* London, Sage (translated by R. Nice).

—— (1979) *The Inheritors: French students and their relation to culture.* London, University of Chicago Press.

Bowles, S. and Gintis, H. (1976) *Schooling in Capitalist America.* New York, Basic Books.

Brennan, J. (1981) 'Preparing Students for Employment', *Studies in Higher Education*, 10, 2, 151–62.

Brosan, G. (1971) 'A Polytechnic Philosophy', *in* G. Brosan *et al.* (eds) *Patterns and Policies in Higher Education.* Harmondsworth, Penguin.

Brown, H. (1977) *Perception, Theory and Commitment: the new philosophy of science.* Chicago, Precedent Publishing Company.

Brown, S. (1973) 'Academic Freedom', *in* S. Brown (ed.) *Philosophers discuss Education.* London, Macmillan.

Brownlie, I. (1971) *Basic Documents on Human Rights.* Oxford, Oxford University Press.

—— (1981) *Basic Documents on Human Rights* (second edition). Oxford, Clarendon Press.

Brubacher, J. (1978) *On the Philosophy of Higher Education.* San Francisco, Jossey-Bass. Revised edition 1982.

Bruner, J. (1977) *The Process of Education.* London, Harvard University Press.

Caine, S. (1969) *British Universities: purpose and prospects.* London, Bodley Head.

Carnegie Foundation for the Advancement of Teaching (1982) *The Control of the Campus.* Princeton, Princeton University Press.

Carreras, J. (1987) *La Relacion Universidad-Sociedad: el consejo social.* Murcia, Direccion Regional de Universidad e Investigacion.

Caudrey, A. (1987) Whose Research?, *New Society*, 23 October, 12–13.

Cavell, S. (1979) *The Claim of Reason.* New York, Oxford University Press.

Chait, R. and Ford, A. (1982) *Beyond Traditional Tenure.* San Francisco, Jossey-Bass.

Chalendar, J. de (1970) *Une Loi pour l'Universite.* Paris, Desdee de Brouwer.

Chapman, J. (1983) *The Western University on Trial.* Berkeley, University of California Press.

Chorley, L. (1964) 'Academic Freedom in the United Kingdom', *in* H. Baade and R. Everett (eds), *Academic Freedom.* Oceana Publications.

Clark, B. (1983) *The Higher Education System: academic organisation in cross-national perspective.* Berkeley, University of California Press.

—— (ed., 1984) *Perspectives on Higher Education: eight disciplinary and comparative views.* Berkeley, University of California Press.

Collins, R. (1979) *The Credential Society.* London, Academic Press.

Committee of Vice-Chancellors & Principals (1985) *Report of the Steering Committee for Efficiency Studies in Universities* (the Jarratt Report). London, CVCP.

—— (1987) *Performance Indicators in Universities: a second statement*. London, CVCP.

—— (1987b) *Circular*, 22 December.

Committee on Higher Education (Robbins) (1963) *Report*. London, HMSO.

Connolly, W. (1981) 'Taylor, Foucault and Otherness', *Political Theory*, 13, 3, 365–76.

Conseil Superieur de la Recherche at de la Technologie (1986) *Rapport Annuel sur l'Evaluation de la Politique Nationale de Recherche et de Developpement Technologique*. Paris.

Council of Europe Newsletter (1986) 'France: projet de loi sur l'enseignement supérieur'. No. 3, 14.

CRE Information (1983) 'On the Perils and Rewards of Boldness'. No. 62.

Denny, T. and Arnold, K. (1987) 'In Career Goals, Female Valedictorians Fall Behind', *New York Times Educational Supplement*, 8 November, 7.

Department of Education and Science (1987a) *Contracts between the Funding Bodies and Higher Education Institutions*. London, DES.

—— (1987b) *Accounting and Auditing in Higher Education*. London, DES.

Doyle, R. and Chickering, A. (1982) 'Crediting Service Learning', *in* S. Goodlad (ed.) *Study Service*. Windsor, NFER/Nelson.

Dziech, B. (1987) Sexual Harassment Workshop, University of Louisville, 14 November.

Dziech, B. and Weiner, L. (1984) *The Lecherous Professor: Sexual Harassment on Campus*. Boston, Beacon Press.

Edwards, E. (1982) *Higher Education for Everyone*. Nottingham, Spokesman.

Epstein, N. (1981) 'When Professors Swap Good Grades for Sex', *The Washington Post*. 6 September, section C, 1.

Eustace, R. (1982) 'British Higher Education and the State', *European Journal of Education*, 17, 3.

—— (1983) 'The Reform of Academic Tenure', *Higher Education Review*, 65–75.

Evans, N. (1981) *The Knowledge Revolution: making the link between learning and work*. London, Grant MacIntyre.

—— (1983) *Curriculum Opportunity: a map of experiential learning in entry requirements to higher and further education award-bearing courses*. London, Further Education Unit.

Farley, L. (1980) *Sexual Shakedown*. New York, Warner Books.

Foucault, M. (1973) *The Order of Things: an archaeology of the human sciences*. New York, Vintage Books.

—— (1977) *Discipline and Punish*. New York, Vintage Books.

—— (1980) *The History of Sexuality*. Volume 1. New York, Vintage Books.

Friedrichs, R. (1972) *A Sociology of Sociology*. New York, Free Press.

Fuchs, R. (1964) 'Academic Freedom: its basic philosophy, function and history', *in* H. Baade and R. Everett (eds) *Academic Freedom*. Oceana Publications.

Galbraith, J. (1969) *The New Industrial State*. Harmondsworth, Penguin.

Gellert, C. (1985) 'State Interventionism and Institutional Autonomy: university development and state interference in England and West Germany', *Oxford Review of Education*, 11, 3, 283–93.

Gellner, E. (1964) 'The Crisis in the Humanities and the Mainstream of Philosophy', *in* J. Plumb (ed.) *The Crisis in the Humanities*. Harmondsworth, Penguin.

—— (1969) *Thought and Change*. London, Weidenfeld and Nicolson.

—— (1980) 'Breaking through the bars of the Rubber Cage', *Times Higher Education Supplement*, 9 May.

Gibbons, M. and Johnson, C. (1982) 'Science, Technology and the Development of the Transistor', *in* Barnes and Edge (eds) *Science in Context*. Milton Keynes, Open University Press.

Goodlad, S. (ed., 1975) *Project Methods in Higher Education*. Guildford, SRHE.
—— (1976) *Conflict and Consensus in Higher Education*. London: Hodder & Stoughton.
—— (ed, 1982) *Study Service*. Windsor, NFER/Nelson.
—— (ed, 1983) *Economies of Scale in Higher Education*. Guildford, SRHE.
Goodlad, S. and Pippard, S. (1982) 'The Curriculum of Higher Education', in D. Bligh (ed.) *Professionalism and Flexibility for Learning*. Guildford, SRHE.
Gouldner, A. (1971) *The Coming Crisis of Western Sociology*. London, Heinemann.
Griffith, J. (1987) 'Muster up the Troops', *Times Higher Education Supplement*, 18 September, 11.
Griffith, J. *et al.* (1972) *The Case for Academic Freedom and Democracy*. London, Council for Academic Freedom and Democracy.
Gruber, K. (1982) 'Higher Education and the State in Austria: an historical and institutional approach', *European Journal of Education*, 17, 3.
Gunnell, J. (1986) *Between Philosophy and Politics*. Amherst, University of Massachusetts Press.
Habermas, J. (1971) *Towards a Rational Society*. London, Heinemann.
Hall, R. and Sandler, B. (1982) *The Classroom Climate: a chilly one for women?* Washington, American Association of Colleges.
—— (1984) *Out of the Classroom: a chilly campus climate for women?* Washington, American Association of Colleges.
—— (1986) *The Campus Climate Revisited: chilly for women faculty, administrators and graduate students*. Washington, American Association of Colleges.
Harding, S. (1986) *The Science Question in Feminism*. Ithaca, Cornell University Press.
Herzog, D. (1985) *Without Foundations: justification in political theory*. Ithaca, Cornell University Press.
Hirst, P. (1974) *Knowledge and the Curriculum*. London, Routledge and Kegan Paul.
—— (1986) 'The Ruskin Row: free speech and solidarity', *New Statesman*, 24 October, 20.
Hofstadter, R. ad Metzger, W. (1955) *The Development of Academic Freedom in the United States*. New York, Columbia University Press.
Hoggart, R. (1958) *The Uses of Literacy*. Harmondsworth, Penguin.
Hook, S. (1970) *Academic Freedom and Academic Anarchy*. Delta.
Hume, D. (1748) *Enquiry Concerning Human Understanding*. Oxford, Clarendon Press (1975 edition).
Humphrey, J. (1984) 'Political and Related Rights', *in* T. Meron (ed.) *Human Rights in International Law*. Oxford, Clarendon Press.
ICED (1987) *The Spanish University Reform: an assessment report*. Madrid.
Ions, E. (1970) 'Threats to Academic Freedom in Britain', *The Critical Quarterly*, Summer, 113–47.
Jadot, J. (1984) 'Structures: outils de pouvoir pour demain', *CRE VIII Assemblee Generale*, Athens.
Kamp, N. (1986) 'Autonomie pour Servir', *Actes de la VIIIe Assemblee Generale de la Conference des Recteurs Europeens*. Geneve, CRE.
Kaplan, C. and Schrecker, E. (eds) (1983) *Regulating the Intellectuals: perspectives on academic freedom in the 1980's*. New York, Praeger.
Kleinig, J. (1982) 'Academic Freedom', *Educational Philosophy and Theory*, 14, 15–25.
Kloss, G. (1985) 'The Academic Restructuring of British and German Universities and Greater Efficiency: a comparative perspective', *Oxford Review of Education*, 11, 3, 271–82.
Kluge, N. (1984) *Studienform in den Lander*. Bonn.
Kogan, M. (1984) 'Implementing Expenditure Cuts in British Higher Education', *in*

R. Premfors (ed.) *Higher Education Organisation: conditions for policy implementation*. Stockholm, Almqvist and Wiksell.

Kunzel, K. (1982) 'The State and Higher Education in the Federal Republic of Germany', *European Journal of Education*, 17, 3.

Leavis, F. (1979) *Education and the University*. Cambridge, Cambridge University Press.

Leroy, P. (1982) 'France: autonomie, modes et réalités', *CRE Information*, 58.

Lord Privy Seal (1971) *A Framework for Government Research and Development*. London, HMSO, Cmnd 4814.

MacIntyre, A. (1981, 1985) *After Virtue*. Indiana, University of Notre Dame Press; London, Duckworth.

MacKinnon, C. (1979) *The Sexual Harassment of Working Women: a case of sex discrimination*. New Haven, Yale University Press.

MacVicar, M. and McGavern, N. (1984) 'Not Only Engineering: the MIT undergraduate research opportunities programme', *in* S. Goodlad (ed.) *Education for the Professions: quis custodiet?* Windsor, SRHE/NFER/Nelson.

Magsino, R. (1978) 'Student Academic Freedom and the Changing Student/University Relationship', *in* K. Strike and K. Egan (eds) *Ethics and Educational Policy*. London, Routledge and Kegan Paul.

Megill, A. (1985) *Prophets of Extremity: Nietzsche, Heidegger, Foucault, Derrida*. Berkeley, University of California Press.

Ministerie van Onderwijs en Weterschappen (1983) *Beleids Voornemens: taakverdeling en concentratioe weterschappelijk onderwijs*. Den Haag.

—— (1985) *Hoger Onderwijs: autonomie en hivaliteit*. Zoetermeer.

Minogue, K. (1973) *The Concept of a University*. London, Weidenfeld and Nicolson.

Moi, T. (1985) *Sexual/Textual Politics*. London, Methuen.

Le Monde-Campus (1987) *Les Eleves-ingenieurs Decouvrent la Recherche*. 15 October, No. 15.

Montefiore, A. (1975) *Neutrality and Impartiality: the university and political commitment*. London, Cambridge University Press.

Moodie, G. (1982) 'Tenure', *Higher Education Review*, 14, 3, 49–55.

Morris, A. (1974) 'Flexibility and the Tenured Academic', *Higher Education Review*, 6, 2, 3–25.

Mullinger, J. (1911) 'Universities', *Encyclopaedia Britannica*. 11th edition, volume xxvii.

National Advisory Body for Local Authority Higher Education (1984) *A Strategy for Higher Education into the late 1980's and beyond*. London, NAB.

—— (1986) *Transferable Skills in Employment: the contribution of higher education*. London, NAB.

—— (1987) *Management for a Purpose: report of the good management practice group*. London, NAB.

Neave, G. (1980) 'Accountability and Control', *European Journal of Education*, 15, 1, 49–60.

—— (1982) 'La Notion de Limite, Modèle des Liens Existants entre l'Université et l'Etat', *CRE Information*, 58, 6–20.

—— (1985) 'Strategic Planning, Reform and Governance in French Higher Education', *Studies in Higher Education*, 10, 1.

—— (1987a) 'European University Systems: part 1', *CRE Information*, 75, 54, 66, 125.

—— (1987b) 'Systemes Universitaires Europeen: 2e partie', *CRE Information*, 77, p. 32.

Neave, G. and Rhoades, G. (1987) 'The Academic Estate in Western Europe', *in* B. Clark (ed.) *The Academic Profession: national, disciplinary and institutional settings*. Berkeley, University of California Press.

Neufield, V. and Chong, J. (1984) 'Problem-based Learning in Medicine', *in* S. Goodlad (ed.) *Education for the Professions: quis custodiet?* Windsor, SRHE/BFER/Nelson.

Newman, J. (1852) *The Idea of a University*. 1976 edition, edited by I. Ker. Oxford, Clarendon Press.

Nozick, R. (1974) *Anarchy, State and Utopia*. Oxford, Blackwell.

NRC Handelsblad (1985) *Commissie voor Visitatie: kamerstemt in met inspectie van universiteiten*.

NUS/NCCL (1970) *Academic Freedom and the Law*.

OECD (1986) *Innovation Policy*. Paris.

O'Hear, A. (1988) *The Element of Fire*. London, Routledge and Kegan Paul.

Passmore, J. (1984) 'Academic Ethics?', *Journal of Applied Philosophy*, 1, 1, 63–77.

Paulsen, F. (1906) *The German Universities and University Study* (translated by F. Thilly and W. Elwang). London, Longmans, Green and Co.

Peacocke, R. and Gillett, G. (eds, 1987) *Persons and Personality: a contemporary inquiry*. Oxford, Blackwell.

Pedro, F. (1988) 'Spain: setting the conditions for an evaluative state', *European Journal of Education*, 23, 1.

Percy, K. and Ramsden, P. (1980) *Independent Study: two examples from English higher education*. Guildford, SRHE.

Perry, W. (1970) *Forms of Intellectual and Ethical Development in the College Years: a scheme*. New York, Holt, Rinehart and Winston.

—— (1981) 'Cognitive and Ethical Growth: the making of meaning', *in* A. Chickering (ed.) *The Modern American College*. San Francisco, Jossey-Bass.

Pincoffs, E. (1975) 'Introduction', *in* E. Pincoffs (ed.) *The Concept of Academic Freedom*. University of Texas Press.

Popper, K. (1962) *Conjectures and Refutations*. New York, Basic Books.

Premfors, R. (1984) 'Analysis in Politics: the regionalisation of Swedish higher education', *Comparative Education Review*, 28.

Rashdall, H. (1895) *The Universities of the Middle Ages*. Oxford, Clarendon Press.

Ravitch, D. (1977) 'The Revisionists Revised: studies in the historiography of American education', *Proceedings of the National Academy of Education*, 4.1, 84.

Rawls, J. (1972) *A Theory of Justice*. Oxford, Clarendon Press.

Reiss, H. (ed., 1987) *Emmanuel Kant: political writings*. Cambridge, Cambridge University Press.

Rendel, M. (1987) 'Women's Equal Right to Equal Education', *in* M. Buckley and M. Anderson (eds) *Women, Equality and Europe*. London, Macmillan.

Robbins, L. (1966) *Academic Freedom*. Inaugural lecture under thank-offering to Britain fund. Oxford, Oxford University Press.

Robertson, C. (1985) *Report on Survey of Sexual Harassment Policies and Procedures*. Bloomington, Office of Women's Affairs, Indiana University.

Rogers, C. (1969) *Freedom to Learn*. Ohio, Charles Merrill.

Rorty, R. (1979) *Philosophy and the Mirror of Nature*. Princeton, Princeton University Press.

Rose, H. and Rose, S. (1976) *The Political Economy of Science*. London, Macmillan.

Sartorius, R. (1975) 'Tenure and Academic Freedom', *in* E. Pincoffs (ed.) *The Concept of Academic Freedom*. University of Texas Press.

Sarup, M. (1978) *Marxism and Education*. London, Routledge and Kegan Paul.

Schrecker, E. (1986) *No Ivory Tower: McCarthyism and the Universities*. New York, Oxford University Press.

Scott, P. (1984) *The Crisis in the University*. London, Croom Helm.

Searle, J. (1972) *The Campus War*. Harmondsworth, Penguin.

Secretary of State for Education and Science *et al.* (1987) *Higher Education: meeting the challenge*. London, HMSO.

Sellars, W. (1963) *Science, Perception and Reality*. New York, Humanities Press.

Sharp, R. (1980) *Knowledge, Ideology and the Politics of Schooling: towards a marxist analysis of education*. London, Routledge and Kegan Paul.

Shils, E. (1983) *The Academic Ethic*. London, University of Chicago Press.

Shils, E. and Daalder H. (eds, 1982) *Politicians, Universities and Bureaucrats*. Cambridge, Cambridge University Press.

Sieghart, P. (1983) *The International Law of Human Rights*. Oxford, Clarendon Press.

Silber, J. (1973) 'Tenure in Context', *in* B. Smith *et al.*, *The Tenure Debate*. San Francisco, Jossey-Bass.

Simon, B. (1964) *Education and the Labour Movement 1870–1918*. London, Lawrence and Wishart.

Skinner, B. (1968) *The Technology of Teaching*. New York, Appleton-Century-Crofts.

Skinner, B. (1971) *Beyond Freedom and Dignity*. New York, Alfred Knopf.

Society for Research into Higher Education (1983) *Excellence in Diversity: towards a new strategy for higher education*. Guildford, SRHE.

Staropouli, P. (1987) 'The National Evaluation Committee', *European Journal of Education*, 22, 2.

Stockman, N. (1983) *Anti-Positivist Theories of Science: critical rationalism, critical theory and scientific realism*. Dordrecht, D. Reidel.

Study Group on Scholarly Freedom and Human Rights (1977) *Scholarly Freedom and Human Rights*. London, Barry Rose.

Svensson, L. (1982) 'The State and Higher Education: a sociological critique from Sweden', *European Journal of Education*, 17, 3.

—— (1987) *Higher Education and the State in Sweden*. Stockholm, Almqvist and Wiksell.

Taylor, C. (1975) 'Neutrality in the University', *in* A. Montefiore (ed.) *Neutrality and Impartiality: the university and political commitment*. London, Cambridge University Press.

—— (1984) 'Foucault on Freedom and Truth', *Political Theory*, 12, 2, 152–83.

Templeman, G. (1982) 'Britain: a model at risk', *CRE Information*, 58.

Tight, M. (1985) 'Academic Freedom Re-examined', *Higher Education Review*, 18, 1, 7–23.

—— (1987) 'The Value of Higher Education: full-time or part-time?', *Studies in Higher Education*, 12, 2, 169–85.

—— (1988) 'Institutional Typologies', *Higher Education Review*, 21.

Tiryakian, E. (1962) *Sociologism and Existentialism*. Englewood Cliffs, Prentice Hall.

Trow, M. (1980) *Dilemmas of Higher Education in the 1980's and 1990's*, Conference of Learned Societies, Montreal (mimeo).

Twitchen, J. (1988) (ed.) *The Black and White Media Show*. 85.

United Kingdom Council of World University Service (1967) *Staff–student Relations*. Conference report.

University Grants Committee (1984) *A Strategy for Higher Education into the 1990's: the University Grants Committee's advice*. London, HMSO.

Vught, F. von (1987) 'A new Autonomy in European Higher Education', *European Association for Institutional Research*, Enschede (mimeo).

Wagner, L. (1982) 'The Challenge of Change', *in* L. Wagner (ed.) *Agenda for Institutional Change in Higher Education*. Guildford, Society for Research into Higher Education.

Wenger, G. (1987, ed.) *The Research Relationship: practice and politics in social policy research*. London, Allen & Unwin.

Willingham, W. (1977) *Principles of Good Practice in Assessing Experiential Learning*. Columbia, CAEL.

Winter, G. (1966) *Elements for a Social Ethic: scientific and ethical perspectives on social process.* New York, Macmillan.

Wolin, S. (1981) 'Max Weber: legitimation, method and the politics of theory', *Political Theory*, 9, 401–24.

Young, I. (1986) 'Impartiality and the Civil Public: some implications of feminist critiques of moral and political theory', *Praxis International*, 5, 4, 381–401.

Young, M. (ed, 1971) *Knowledge and Control: new directions for the sociology of education.* London, Collier-Macmillan.

Index

The Society for Research into Higher Education

The Society exists both to encourage and co-ordinate research and development into all aspects of Higher Education, including academic, organizational and policy issues; and also to provide a forum for debate, verbal and printed. Through its activities, it draws attention to the significance of research into, and development in, Higher Education and to the needs of scholars in this field. (It is not concerned with research generally, except, for instance, as a subject of study.)

The Society's income derives from subscriptions, book sales, conferences and specific grants. It is wholly independent. Its corporate members are institutions of higher education, research institutions and professional, industrial, and governmental bodies. Its individual members include teachers and researchers, administrators and students. Members are found in all parts of the world and the Society regards its international work as amongst its most important activities.

The Society discusses and comments on policy, organizes conferences and encourages research. Under the Imprint SRHE & OPEN UNIVERSITY PRESS, it is a specialist publisher, having some 40 titles in print. It also publishes *Studies in Higher Education* (three times a year) which is mainly concerned with academic issues, *Higher Education Quarterly* (formerly *Universities Quarterly*) which will be mainly concerned with policy issues, *Research into Higher Education Abstracts* (three times a year), and a *Bulletin* (six times a year).

The Society's committees, study groups and branches are run by members (with help from a small staff at Guildford), and aim to provide a form for discussion. The groups at present include a Teacher Education Study Group, a Staff Development Group, a Women in Higher Education Group and a Continuing Education Group which may have had their own organization, subscriptions or publications; (eg the *Staff Development Newsletter*). The Governing Council, elected by members, comments on current issues; and discusses policies with leading figures, notably at its evening Forums. The Society organizes seminars on current research for officials of DES and other ministries, an Anglo-American series on standards, and is in touch with bodies in the UK such as the NAB, CVCP, UGC, CNAA and the British Council, and with sister-bodies overseas. Its current research projects include one on the relationship between entry qualifications and degree results, directed by Prof. W.D. Furneaux (Brunel) and one on questions of quality directed by Prof. G.C. Moodie (York). A project on the evaluation of the research standing of university departments is in preparation. The Society's conferences are often held jointly. Annual Conferences have considered 'Professional Education' (1984). 'Continuing Education' (1985, with Goldsmiths' College) 'Standards and Criteria in Higher Education' (1986, with Bulmershe CHE), 'Restructuring' (1987, with the City of Birmingham Polytechnic) and 'Academic Freedom' (1988, the University of Surrey). Other conferences have considered the DES 'Green Paper' (1985, with the Times Higher Education Supplement), and 'The First-Year Experience' (1986, with the University of South Carolina and Newcastle Polytechnic). For some of the Society's conferences, special studies are commissioned in advance, as 'Precedings'.

Members receive free of charge the Society's *Abstracts*, annual conference Proceedings (or 'Precedings'), *Bulletin and International Newsletter* and may buy SRHE & OPEN UNIVERSITY PRESS books at booksellers' discount. Corporate members also receive the Society's journal *Studies in Higher Education* free (individuals at a heavy discount). They may also obtain *Evaluation Newsletter* and certain other journals at a discount, including the NFER *Register of Educational Research*. There is a substantial discount to members, and to staff of corporate members, on annual and some other conference fees.